The Elephant of Silence

The Elephant
of Silence

ESSAYS ON POETICS AND CINEMA

John Wall Barger

Louisiana State University Press
Baton Rouge

Published by Louisiana State University Press
lsupress.org

LSU Press Paperback Original

DESIGNER: Mandy McDonald Scallan
TYPEFACE: Sentinel

Cover illustration courtesy Unsplash (Nathan Dumlao).

Cataloging-in-Publication Data are available at the Library of
Congress.

ISBN 978-0-8071-8157-7 (paperback) | ISBN 978-0-8071-8206-2
(epub) | ISBN 978-0-8071-8207-9 (pdf)

Imaginez ce que pourrait être le cinéma des poètes.

—Jean Cocteau

Contents

Preface &
Acknowledgments

These essays began, slowly, as fragments and notes about art, focusing on questions that I didn't know how to answer. *Why do I like "cold" art, such as the poems of Louise Glück and the films of Stanley Kubrick, so much? What does it mean for an artist to really* look *at something? What does Lorca mean by "the deep song," and why do some poems and films tap into it, while others do not?* These questions led me toward language and ideas I wasn't sure how to define: Lorca's *duende*, Nabokov's *poshlost*, Bashō's *underglimmer*, Huizinga's *ludic*, Tarkovsky's *Zona*, and others.

Over and over, each essay—using contemporary poems and art house films as lenses—led me scratching and clawing toward what Seamus Heaney might have meant when he said "you're after something just at the edge of your knowledge." I discovered that my fascination lies in what I can't describe. It might seem ironic for essays—which must use words, description, explication—to be about silence and listening and watching, but that's where the art I admired guided me. As Mary Ruefle says, "listening is a kind of knowledge, or as close as one can come." Running out of words, I found myself reaching, with trepidation, for philosophical and "spiritual" answers.

If anything, this book is about not knowing. Learning to be an artist, and a viewer of art, in the Keatsian spirit of "being in uncertainties, Mysteries, doubts, without any irritable reaching after fact and reason." In the famous last scene of Fellini's *La dolce vita,* Marcello (Mastroianni) is at a party on the beach at dawn, when the partygoers discover a dead manta ray. A critic might be tempted to interpret this *mostro* (monster), as they call it, as the final response to the existential questions the director has been asking throughout the film (*Q:* is the second coming imminent? *A:* dead fish). But the fish is also just a fish. Fellini, refusing to reconcile what it should mean to us, leaves it mysterious: part symbol, maybe, or just a dead thing for the hungover Romans to talk about.

I'm a poet and cinephile, not an academic. As such, these essays chug forward through an accumulation of comparisons, analogies of unlike things rubbed together, as I attempt to inch toward impossible definitions. Adding and adding, listening, following. Hacking, at times, through the forest of ideas. We cannot force the best poems or films into a single box, but if we keep our focus on them, and ask questions, we can catch their glimmers and glints.

All art is conversation. These essays grew out of conversations with friends, poets, artists, students, my mother—in workshops, classrooms, living rooms, barrooms. And from reading, and from drinking in art in many forms, which are also conversations. While reading Blake's "The Tyger," I can't help but converse with the long-dead poet; I'd love to know what kind of "furnace" he thinks the tiger's brain comes from!

The first of these essays were written in Dharamsala, north India, where my wife Tiina and I lived from 2014 to 2017, and the rest in West Philadelphia, where we now live. It's been a gradual, arduous, seven or eight years, seeking the weight in these. I had, first, to wriggle free of my learned notions of what an essay should be and just let these be discursive in logic and organic in form. This is not a book that explains or defines poetry or film, or aims to win people over to these genres. I'm not offering a way to write poems or watch films. Unless not knowing can be thought of as a way.

I'm grateful to the editors of the following publications, in which essays from this book originally appeared, though sometimes in slightly different form: *Full Stop:* "In Praise of the Goblin"; *Poetry Northwest:* "The Underglimmer" and "The Music of the Zone"; *Literary Matters:* "In the Cold Theater of the Poem" and "Club Silencio"; *Cleaver:* "The Elephant of Silence."

This book would not exist without the generous extended feedback of certain brilliant folks I'm lucky enough to know: Stephanie Bolster, Ryan Wilson, Cameron MacKenzie, Ben Gallagher, Raphael Krut-Landau, Jean Barger, Tiina Rosenqvist. Others have encouraged these essays in uncountable ways: Sun Man Ho, Blair Reeve, Micheline Maylor, Stephanie Yorke, Emily Alex, Bill Carty, Mark Danowsky, Zach Savich. I'm grateful to the Hambidge Center, where I wrote the first drafts of the "Elephant of Silence" essay while I was artist in residence, in June 2020. My thanks to James W. Long at LSU Press for believing in this book and supporting it at every stage. And to Tiina for suggesting—softly, one afternoon, on a walk on a dirt road in Dharamsala—that such a book might be possible.

The Elephant of Silence

IN PRAISE OF THE GOBLIN

This "mysterious power that all may feel and no philosophy can explain," is, in sum, the earth-force, the same *duende* that fired the heart of Nietzsche, who sought it in its external forms on the Rialto Bridge, or in the music of Bizet, without ever finding it, or understanding that the *duende* he pursued had rebounded from the mystery-minded Greeks to the Dancers of Cádiz or the gored, Dionysian cry of Silverio's *Siguiriya*.
  —Federico García Lorca

All love songs must contain *duende*. For the love song is never truly happy.
  —Nick Cave

Perhaps some remember the first time they were exposed to images of violence and death. For me, it's hazy. It might have been the art house movies, some R-rated, that my parents brought me to back in the 1970s. I remember Australian New Wave films like *Picnic at Hanging Rock* and *The Last Wave*. And *The Chant of Jimmie Blacksmith,* about an Aboriginal man wronged by society who goes on a murderous rampage, killing white folks. That night I tossed and turned in bed, soaked in sweat. I had a similar response to *Easy Rider.* The last scene when Dennis Hopper and Peter Fonda are shotgunned on their motorcycles. My father resembled those marvelous hippies and also rode a motorcycle.

Or was it, perhaps, when my mother read me Roald Dahl's short stories? In the middle of "The Swan," from *The Wonderful Story of Henry Sugar and Six More,* she paused at the point where a boy with a rifle is savagely bullying another boy. The bully ties the boy to railway tracks, almost killing him. Later the bully shoots a swan, cuts off its wings, ties them to the boy. Did my mother, while pausing, ask herself if the terrifying narrative—classified as YA fiction—was appropriate for me? That swan, both dead and alive, is still lodged in my mind.

I'm grateful that my parents allowed me to absorb such a diversity of potent art when I was impressionable. In that fertile soil, my love for a certain type of art grew. Art smeared in mud and blood. Art that's impolite. That surprises with its capacity for pain. That shocks and triggers us—as Roland Barthes describes the *punctum* in his favorite photographs, in *Camera Lucida*—with a "sting, speck, cut, little hole." When I got older, I realized there's a name for this aesthetic.

The famous lecture *"Juego y teoría del duende"* ("Theory and Play of the *Duende*")—which Lorca wrote while on board the transatlantic ship *Conte Grande,* and presented at a conference in Buenos Aires, October, 1933—is about a goblin called *duende.* Lorca explains that *duende* is not an angel or a muse, both of which are far too polite, but rather, a "mysterious power." A goblin that "will not approach at all if he does not see the possibility of death, if he is not convinced he will circle death's house."

I knew this goblin. I felt the frisson of it passing through me while listening to Merry Clayton's voice as it cracks on the word "murder" in the Rolling Stones' "Gimme Shelter." In the Sex Pistols' jarring, driving guitar in "God Save the Queen." In Jimi Hendrix's rendition of "The Star-Spangled Banner" at Woodstock: that warped national anthem morphing into an onslaught of bombs dropped on Vietnam. In Nirvana's MTV Unplugged performance of "Where Did You Sleep Last Night": out of the whining lover Cobain, the howling cuckold *duende* suddenly bursts forth.

In Dennis Hopper's middle finger at the rednecks who shoot him.

It's the goblin that entered Emily Dickinson's room when she felt "physically as if the top of [her] head were taken off."

Lorca respected fear, anger, anguish, joy—the range of raw human feelings—but scorned reason: "intellect is oftentimes the foe of poetry," he said, "because it imitates too much, it elevates the poet to a throne of acute angles and makes him forget that in time the ants can devour him, too, or that a great arsenical locust can fall on his head." Intellect might capture a thin notion of strife, but the goblin inhabits the struggle bodily. "The *duende* . . . is a power and not a construct, is a struggle and not a concept. I have heard an old guitarist, a true virtuoso, remark, 'The *duende* is not in the throat, the *duende* comes up from inside, up from the very soles of the feet.'"

The speaker of Lorca's four-part elegy "Lament for Ignacio Sánchez Mejías"—brokenhearted over the death of his close friend, a famous matador who died in the bullring in 1934—gushes with grief and longing and song. Trapped in his wound.

> I will not see it!

> Tell the moon to come
> for I do not want to see the blood
> of Ignacio on the sand.

> I will not see it!

> The moon wide open.
> Horse of still clouds,
> and the grey bull ring of dreams
> with willows in the barreras.

I will not see it!

Let my memory kindle!
Warm the jasmines
of such minute whiteness!

I will not see it!

The cow of the ancient world
passed her sad tongue
over a snout of blood
spilled on the sand,
and the bulls of Guisando,
partly death and partly stone,
bellowed like two centuries
sated with treading the earth.
No.
I do not want to see it!
I will not see it!
   —from Part 2, "The Spilled Blood"

He wants the moon to come to take away the terrible vision of
Ignacio's blood. With the moon comes a dream of a monolithic cow
lapping the bullfighter's blood with her "sad tongue." The pain is
overwhelming, for him and for us. His exclamation "I will not see
it!"—evoking the women belting out *siguiriyas,* and the "gored,
Dionysian cry" of Merry Clayton—is a kind of *jaleo:* a chorus in flamenco in which dancers stomp their feet and singers shout and clap
their cupped hands to the rhythm of the song. It's also the *Olé, Olé!*
of bullfights. Lorca's poems, with their repetitions and cries, are
often sung to music.

"Lament" is one of Lorca's most renowned poems perhaps because
the suffering reaches such a dramatic pitch. It's visceral, cryptic,
and bold. Its form—the urgency, surreality, sincerity—borrows from

ancient Hispano-Arabic tropes rooted in Andalusian culture. Lorca's aesthetic stemmed from his worship of the "deep song" of the Spanish Gitanos, or Roma people. "The Roma," he said, "is the most basic, most profound, the most aristocratic of my country, as representative of their way and whoever keeps the flame, blood, and the alphabet of the universal Andalusian truth." Lorca cherished bullfighters, flamenco dancers, and Gitano motifs like horsemen, wolves, blood on the lips, a knife in the heart.

Certainly a film like *Carmen* (1983)—director Carlos Saura's flamenco adaptation of Bizet's opera—feels as though it "comes up from inside, up from the very soles of the feet." In a seminal scene, called "La Tabacalera," two women—ferocious Carmen and Cristina—confront each other, taking long steps back and forth, singing and holding eye contact, like wolves. "In this factory," sings Cristina, "there are more bitches than good girls." Carmen replies, "Don't you annoy Carmen!" and, snatching a knife from a table, cuts Cristina's throat.

Tracy K. Smith, in her essay "Survival in Two Worlds at Once: Federico Garcia Lorca and Duende" argues that we poets can't assume that the goblin will roost in our art. If there's *duende* in our poems, it's a happy accident, a result of living in such a way that makes the goblin curious enough to visit. She loves the concept of *duende,* she says, because it supposes that we don't write poems to win the reader's approval:

> we write poems in order to engage in the perilous yet necessary struggle to inhabit ourselves—our real selves, the ones we barely recognize—more completely. It is then that the duende beckons, promising to impart "something newly created, like a miracle," then it winks inscrutably and begins its game of feint and dodge, lunge and parry, goad and shirk. . . . You'll get your miracle, but only if you can decipher the music of the battle, only if you're willing to take risk after risk.

If we write poems that face our unique struggles, attempting to find "our real selves," *duende* might grant us a "miracle": that is, the poem. *Duende,* it seems, doesn't care who the artist is or what they believe, but only that the work reeks of *human struggle.* Of feelings exposed. Of the "bare, forked animal" smeared in blood and mud.

In a poem Jack Gilbert remembers a woman at a long-ago barbecue: not her name or face, but how, after tearing into a piece of meat, she "wiped the grease on her breasts."

Duende is also a useful panhandle for helping us, as critics of art, to find language to "pick up" unwieldy, ineffable work. As we talk about *duende,* the discussion moves away from the "genius" of the artist and toward what the artwork gives off, as if of its own accord. Picasso was brilliant, sure, but not all of his work has *duende.*

The discussion moves from psychology to myth: as the painter paints, the goblin creeps in the nearby shadows, waiting to catch a whiff of the deep song. If it isn't drawn to the work, it creeps away.

The Polish film *The Cremator* (1969), directed by Juraj Herz, is a deeply unsettling comedy. The main character, Karel Kopfrkingl, is a quirky fellow who works at a crematorium in Prague in the 1930s. At the start, he simply takes his job too seriously. Then he begins collaborating with antisemites, killing off his family, and by the end he turns into a mass murderer who runs the ovens at Nazi extermination camps.

The original novel by Ladislav Fuks that caught Herz's eye is called *Spalovač mrtvol* (*The Burner of Corpses*).

Lorca tells us that *duende* will not come to the artist "if he does not see the possibility of death." But what do *we,* as artists, know about death?

The director, Herz, was Jewish. A concentration camp survivor.

For the first hour of *The Cremator,* I could feel a grin on my face. It's satirical, funny. Kopfrkingl has a big round bland head, with a wry Peter Lorre grin. By turns playful, lascivious, murderous.

Herz's milieu is experimental: Czech New Wave. Faces are shown too closely, with creases and sweat. Kopfrkingl loves to stare into a convex mirror and chat to himself. The film is a kind of long inner monologue by Kopfrkingl, interrupted a few times by others. Scenes blend into one another through Kopfrkingl: zoom in on his face at a restaurant, pan out in a shop full of mirrors. The framing decisions—by Herz and cinematographer Stanislav Milota—are eccentric: juxtaposing Kopfrkingl and his family with animals in a cage. Extreme close-ups, fish-eye lenses, restless inter-cuts. All stark black and white.

The Cremator (1969). Kopfrkingl creepily touches the shoulder of Mrs. Lišková, a cleaner at the crematorium.

Kopfrkingl is likable, to a degree. It's fun to follow him as he cleans his ears, drums up business for his crematorium, flirts awkwardly with women, visits a brothel, listens to Dvořák at full blast. Always with his little grin. He's a creepy dude with a sense of humor, like someone we knew in high school. A morbid Everyman.

His wife, Lakmé, who watches Kopfrkingl with increasing astonishment, goes along with everything he does right up until he hangs her from the bathroom ceiling.

Kopfrkingl carries around a cumbersome book about Tibet, with a photo of the Potala Palace in Lhasa on the cover. He has a vague notion that as a cremator he helps to "liberate" souls. In a baroque ballroom, he delivers a speech about funerals to baffled-looking locals. "In 75 minutes," he purrs, "Miss Čárská will be turned to ashes and fill her urn. But not her soul. That doesn't go in the urn. It will be liberated. 'Reincarnated,' as the Tibetans say. It will rise up into the ether." No matter how morbid the subject matter, his voice retains its hypnotic calm:

> Such a crematorium, dear friends, is pleasing to the Lord, helping him to hasten our transformation into dust. Some people object . . . saying Christ was buried, not cremated. But that's quite another matter. I always tell those good people that they embalmed Our Savior, wrapped him in linen, and buried him in a cave. But no one will bury you in a cave or wrap you in linen. . . . [W]e live in a good and humanitarian state that provides crematoria . . . so that, after life's many tribulations, people may lie down and turn quietly to dust.

Kopfrkingl is followed throughout the film by Death, in the form of a young woman with long black hair parted in the middle. In the final scene, Kopfrkingl is being driven in the pouring rain toward his future role with the Nazis. While he sinks deep into his delusion ("No one will suffer," he whispers. "I shall save them all"), the female apparition—who's kept her distance, watching him impassively—breaks into a mad sprint after his car.

Out of the Prague rain, Potala Palace materializes before the car, growing bigger, as if Kopfrkingl were arriving there. A chorus of ethereal angels sing. *KONEC,* the end.

Duende requires a transformation. An ethos disrupted. For Herz, Kopfrkingl is an agent of change. At first, he's just a petit bourgeois oddball. He takes his wife and children on an excursion to a carnival, finding himself at a wax museum exhibiting grisly murder scenes, severed heads, body parts. "What a scourge," he says, staring at each diseased body, his eyes bright with excitement. After an old friend of his, Reinke, suggests that Kopfrkingl's blood is German and not Czechoslovakian, Kopfrkingl's delusions of grandeur turn to antisemitism. He—initially a doting father, then cold and aloof—turns against his partly Jewish family. We watch his megalomania transform, step by step, into Nazism.

The goblin mutates, shifts, restless, protean, a river reflecting light. Hendrix's guitar whines the national anthem, then bursts with bombs upon Saigon. Kopfrkingl himself, in keeping with his idea of death and the embalming of Christ, transforms the people around him "to dust" before our eyes. We see a ripple effect around him: Prague is pitilessly altered by his presence.

Lorca described *duende*'s power of transformation in a parable:

> Some years ago, in a dancing contest at Jerez de la Frontera, an old lady of eighty, competing against beautiful women and young girls with waists as supple as water, carried off the prize merely by the act of raising her arms, throwing back her head, and stamping the little platform with a blow of her feet; but in the conclave of muses and angels foregathered there—beauties of form and beauties of smile—the dying *duende* triumphed as it had to, trailing the rusted knife blades of its wings along the ground.

Equipment for incinerating as many people as possible

Kopfrkingl being interviewed by a Nazi leader in front of the right panel of Bosch's *Garden of Earthly Delights.*

By the end, Kopfrkingl has morphed into a vision of terror, solidified by a moment of unforgettable framing. He stands in the elaborate office of a Nazi superior who offers him a job as technical supervisor for "the gas furnaces of the future." The camera, slowly panning a long mirrored table, arrives at Kopfrkingl in front of an enormous painting: the right panel of Hieronymus Bosch's *Garden of Earthly Delights,* with its graphic depiction of hell.

In fact, not *in front* of that grotesque nightmare. Within it.

Aesthetically speaking, a wound needs a body.

The painter Francis Bacon would have agreed, I think. Although Bacon lived in an era ruled by abstract expressionists such as Willem de Kooning and Barnett Newman, his work remained stubbornly grounded in the body.

Bacon shows us bodies in jeopardy. His paintings—with their vulnerable and brutal human figures, their guns, nails, syringes, raw meat—

are involuntary convulsions, mutilations, as in the grainy horror films of the '70s such as *Eraserhead, Halloween,* and *Carrie.* "The entire series of spasms in Bacon," says Gilles Deleuze in *Francis Bacon: The Logic of Sensation,* "is of this type: scenes of love, of vomiting and excreting, in which the body attempts to escape from itself *through* one of its organs in order to rejoin the field or material structure."

While figures painted by certain artists—such as Chaïm Soutine, whose *Page Boy at Maxim's* (1927) depicts a misshapen blood-red bellboy with blacked-out eyes—seem to *want* to turn themselves inside out, Bacon's figures, in the psychic space he allows them, actually *do* twist inside out.

Have you ever seen those guilty-dog videos on YouTube, where the dog has eaten an entire pizza off the table, and their human is waving the pizza box, taunting the poor creature—"Did *you* do this, boy? *Did* you?"—and the dog is so mortified that it bares its teeth and distends its face, as if trying to climb out of its own face?

Imagine that grotesque shame, that desire to escape violently from oneself, taken to a pathological degree, and depicted on canvas over and over for a lifetime.

In Bacon's *Study for Self-Portrait* (1964), a figure sits on a bed in a painfully strained, contorted position. The painting emanates a violent, eerie otherness. As viewers, we have a natural impulse to empathize with a figure in pain. To console them. Bacon disrupts these impulses, which creates tension, struggle. First, the figure in *Study for Self-Portrait* is two people: Bacon's head and Lucian Freud's body. Second, the room contains characteristically impossible elements: namely, a bizarre black box hovering in the air behind the head, with a spatter of sinister black mist around it. Third, as the title reveals, it's not a self-portrait but a "Study" for a self-portrait.

Perhaps Bacon, by creating this triple-otherness, is revealing what an alien experience it was for him to look at himself. "It is not I," Deleuze says, "who attempts to escape from my body, it is the body that attempts to escape from itself by means of . . . a spasm: the body as plexus, and its effort or waiting for a spasm."

What seizes our attention, foregrounded by the impossible box behind the head, is the face which seems to be attempting to turn itself inside out. The goblin is everywhere in the room, but surfaces—as if climbing *out* of the body to greet us—from that face which, like Kopfrkingl in front of the Bosch painting, transforms or, yes, *spasms* before our eyes: the left side red and pink, the right disintegrating into ash. Broken, twisted, nightmarish. Bacon's dream of Lynch's Elephant Man. That riveting face is our focus. The locus of struggle and transformation. "The shadow," as Deleuze says, "escapes from the body like an animal we had been sheltering."

Bacon wants us transfixed by the disaster of the face. He gives us no reprieve. No *out*.

The background of Bacon's painting—the bed, walls, room—is just a suggestion, an outline designed to draw our eyes over and over to the face that writhes before us. The goblin requires instability and struggle, which, in this painting, manifest in the grotesque face.

As viewers we long to avert our eyes but can't. We are trapped—like the painter himself, perhaps—in a space of ruthless and harrowing interiority.

Once we've viewed Bacon's work, it's hard to shake the ghastly trauma of it.

I wonder, does the traumatized artist, seeing the wound wherever they look, project it onto their work for the rest of their lives? Frida Kahlo said, "I don't paint dreams or nightmares, I paint my own reality." If Bacon was doomed to repeatedly paint his traumatic reality, how can such work be cathartic or uplifting for us viewers?

For the traumatized person, as Bessel van der Kolk describes in *The Body Keeps the Score,* trauma remains in present tense: "Being traumatized means continuing to organize your life as if the trauma were still going on—unchanged and immutable—as every new encounter or event is contaminated by the past." When a traumatized soldier is triggered, a long-ago explosion feels like it's happening over and over, *right now.*

If an artist is stuck in such a cycle—perhaps allowing the trauma to surface in their work—is that a healthy process for us viewers, who experience what the art expresses by proxy, like secondhand smoke? Is the gored, Dionysian cry of Silverio's *Siguiriya* good for us?

Is it perhaps useful for us, since so many of us are traumatized, to experience the trauma of another in the comparatively safe space of a work of art?

Is there a toxic goblin and a nontoxic goblin? What would Lorca say? Certainly, Bacon's paintings fit Lorca's criteria for *duende:* they're gritty, death-haunted, irrational, with a smidge of the fiendish or unholy. Would Lorca argue that the flamenco chorus that shouts and claps the *jaleo* is purer, sweeter, more spiritual than Bacon's monstrous twisted figures? "In all Andalusia, from the rock of Jaen to the shell of Cádiz, people constantly speak of the *duende* and find it in everything that springs out of energetic instinct. That marvelous singer, 'El Lebrijano,' originator of the *Debla,* observed, 'Whenever I am singing with *duende,* no one can come up to me.'"

To my ear, the ethos of this "marvelous singer" does sound sweeter than that of Bacon's paintings. But, at their base, haven't El Lebrijano and Bacon both tapped into the same "energetic instinct"?

Or are these the wrong questions? Perhaps we should ask, Does artwork really *need* to uplift us? Can't it just be what it *is,* even if it's grotesque, degrading, painful?

Which of the goblin's myriad forms will appear in our own artwork?

"The *duende,*" says Lorca, "works on the body of the dancer like the wind works on sand. With magical force, it converts a young girl into a lunar paralytic; or fills with adolescent blushes a ragged old man begging handouts in the wineshops."

Had my mother not read me the gruesome Roald Dahl story, would I have written one terrifying swan poem after the next?

A man kills a swan at a public park, stuffs the limp corpse into his backpack, cooks and serves it to his friends for dinner, telling them it's chicken. Years later he revisits the park with his daughter, as the miserable dead watch from a nearby building. His daughter is under a spell at the edge of a pond, as a large swan emerges over her. She and the swan are screaming.

Leda is minding her business beside a lake when a swan surges above her like an alien mothership, a Manhattan-sized chandelier shimmering with owls and goblins and at the center is Leda herself, her brightest self, black hair, eyes furious. This gyring swan-earthquake rumbling out of the past toward eternity enters her.

You're trying to tell me you *don't* think of swans as nightmare creatures?

Poems with *duende* are wolves among us. The biblical expression "wolf in sheep's clothing" is meant to warn: Beware of false prophets. Stay away from bad teachers. Be wary, don't fall for it.

But the goblin, far from a bad teacher, is truth on wheels. A sibyl in the living room.

We are so used to hearing the same ideas bleated at us, the same ways, over and over—*Baaa-baaa-baaa, Baaa-baaa-baaa*—that when the goblin arrives in sheep's clothing, it speaks a language so fresh we almost can't register what it's saying. Language supercharged with the energy of a god, like Zeus in his horrible bird costume.

A line trots up to me sidelong in the field and sings—

Brag, sweet tenor bull, / descant on Rawthey's madrigal, / each pebble its part / for the fells' late spring.
    —Basil Bunting

Some lines knock me over as I'm munching the grass—

In tenth grade, I kissed a guy who called me a faggot once or twice a week. / I still see his voice: / six hummingbirds nailed to a wall.
    —Eduardo C. Corral

Some lines shiver with guileless fragility—

Yes, Father! Yes, and always, Yes!
    —Saint Francis de Sales' prayer

Some lines bleat like all the sheep at once—

In the increasingly convincing darkness / The words become palpable, like a fruit / That is too beautiful to eat.
    —John Ashbery

Some lines sound like the shepherd—

And now it seems to me the beautiful uncut hair of graves.
   —Walt Whitman (his answer to the child who asks, "What is the
     grass?")

And some lines sound like the field—

A rotted swan / is hurrying away from the plane-crash mess of her
wings / one here / one there . . .
   —Alice Oswald

The first time I heard Amiri Baraka's electrified performance of his
poem "Dope" was at a community workshop on Baltimore Avenue in
West Philadelphia. Poet Warren C. Longmire played us a recording
of it. A long, stunned silence followed. Here's the beginning:

uuuuuuuuu

uuuuuuuuu
uuuuuuuuu uuu ray light morning fire lynch yet
               uuuuuuu, yester-pain in dreams
               comes again. race-pain, people our people
                  our people
               everywhere . . . yeh . . . uuuuu, yeh
               uuuuu. yeh
               our people
               yes people
               every people
               most people
               uuuuuu, yeh uuuuu, most people
               in pain
               yester-pain, and pain today

(Screams) ooowow! ooowow! It must be
   the devil
(jumps up like a claw stuck him) oooo
   wow! oooowow! (screams)

In Baraka's poem we hear the ecstatic exclamations ("ooowow!")—so
much like the *Olé!* and claps of the *jaleo*—which also sound like cries
of pain from living in a Black body in America. Wound and celebra-
tion together.

Baraka echoes the voice of an Uncle Tom–like Black parishioner
sermonizing on the violence against their community. Rather than
blaming the real culprits—politicians, the news, imperialism, capi-
talism, white folks—the poem's speaker says, "It must be / the devil,"
and gaslights the community itself. By taking on the voice of an un-
discerning churchgoer, Baraka indicts the complacent values of the
church: "yessuh, yessuh, yessuh, yessuh, / put yr money in the plate,
dont be late / . . . you gonna be in / heaven after you die . . . "

The title "Dope" suggests illegal drugs, such as cocaine, brought into
poor Black neighborhoods by the CIA in the '80s, resulting in the addiction and imprisonment of many, especially Black men. This is just
one in a multitude of insults the Black community has endured since
the first ships sailed here from Africa. It's the original sin of America.
The ungraspable emotional truth of the last four hundred years.

For a poet like Baraka, I think, art was a way to broach a subject that's
so hot it feels like it will burn us alive if we touch it. The *duende* of
Baraka's poem, or what the *duende* speaks to, is slavery. Giving voice
to the struggle of Black Americans, Baraka empowers the goblin, as
Lorca says, "to baptize in dark water all those who behold it." "Dope"
certainly does not exonerate those who "behold" it, but provides a
kind of shadow of the original experience, leading the reader, one
would hope, toward empathy and commiseration.

For us viewers, art is a way to *hold,* so to speak, the violence and horror of the world: that is, to experience it in a way that won't destroy us. We can—if we're lucky enough to live free, to some degree, from the turmoil that so much of the artwork I've cited describes— close the book, turn off the TV, walk out of the cinema, go about our day. We can sometimes even grasp an emotional truth that's been eluding us.

Although we can certainly talk about the goblin, it eschews a precise definition. If *duende* has a form at all, it's not, as Lorca makes clear, any of the tropes we might expect:

> I would not have you confuse the *duende* with the theological demon of doubt at whom Luther, on a Bacchic impulse, hurled an inkwell in Nuremberg, or with the Catholic devil, destructive, but short on intelligence, who disguised himself as a bitch to enter the convents, or with the talking monkey that Cervantes' mountebank carried in the comedy about jealousy and the forests of Andalusia.

Here, to comic effect, Lorca tells us what *duende* is not, employing *via negativa,* the mode that John of the Cross used to inch toward a definition of an indefinable God.

Lorca tells us that *duende* is a flying goblin but warns that there is "neither map nor discipline" for anyone foolish enough to try to pin it down further. He's fascinated not by the appearance of *duende,* but by the effects of the goblin on those possessed by it. "Enough to know that he kindles the blood like an irritant, that he exhausts, that he repulses, all the bland, geometrical assurances, that he smashes the styles; that he makes of a Goya, master of the grays, the silvers, the roses of the great English painters, a man painting with his knees and his fists in bituminous blacks."

The goblin arrives *through* people, not in front of them. More poltergeist than monster. We can't know its specific form, but we see it appear—fluidly, over and over again—in what we fear, and where that fear ignites into inspiration.

For each of us it manifests differently. For Nick Cave, as violent cowboy songs. For Juraj Herz, as Kopfrkingl and his female death-shadow. In Mayan and Mestizo folklore, as a three-foot-tall creature—ugly, stumpy, hairy, thumbless, feet pointing backward—called *Tata Duende*.

Once, in a poetry workshop, a student of mine said that *duende* reminded them of Jenova Chen's 2008 video game *Flower*. I looked it up. The player drifts across a vast open world, touching flowers that burst into blossom, transforming a desiccated desert into a pastoral jungle. I think Lorca would have loved it.

"*Duende?*" said the poet Zach Savich, softly, over a beer with me one evening, "Is that when a shadow falls across a thing?" That stuck with me. For, yes, a shadow does not make a thing disappear, but just casts it in a different light. If darkness is death itself, a shadow is just a hint, or vision, of death. The shadow, falling across a thing we thought was ours, shakes us from our dream of invulnerability and eternal life, reminding us that everything around us—car, house, country, family, possessions—is transient. Perishable.

And in that shadow of fear and denial, the goblin giggles and twirls and prances and stomps his feet. As if mocking us!

THE UNDERGLIMMER

I. THE FIRST GATE

In The Woodlands Cemetery in West Philadelphia, there's one oak tree that's taller, broader than the others.

It's November, 2021. Yesterday the tree's leaves were bright red. Last night it rained and today its leaves are in the grass. All summer I've watched people watching this tree, making little awestruck sounds. Some took selfies with it. Others ate lunch or did yoga under it. Once, while I was sitting under it, an old woman appeared beside me looking up at two hawks circling.

We're in month twenty of the Covid pandemic. Three-quarters of a million Americans are dead. I, like many I know, have been feeling an encroaching sense of dread. It's a lonely, isolated time; all of us in masks, keeping our distance. One point of respite, where we can commiserate, is social media. But I've become hopelessly addicted, checking my emails and notifications every minute of the day.

My ability to concentrate has suffered from social media's demand for quick results and rewards. Even out on a walk, rather than looking at the terrain around me, I'm formulating posts for later. To combat this, I've limited myself to one hour of social media per day. And I take daily walks to The Woodlands to look at the oak tree, and do not post about it.

As I slow down and look at the oak, day after day, it changes. Yesterday it was a Gustav Klimt painting: lush, golden, teeming. Today it's an Egon Schiele drawing: gaunt, braced for winter. Some days it reaches up eight thousand arms. On others it bows, an acolyte. Over time the tree has become part of my mental landscape. I've absorbed it into my broader, archetypal story of the earth.

Through the tree I'm learning to look again. When I unleash my mind upon it, sustaining my gaze, something happens. I see the seed it came from, and the mulch where it goes when it dies. And I see its opposite: the broken bottle, the truck coughing smoke, the fizzing electrical wires. I see my own body: my nervous system, my bones. My brain a tree, a cauliflower of existence. There is a growing between mind and tree. Blood coursing through the eye, chlorophyll pulsing in the cells of the leaves. Back and forth.

The tree reads me. Embeds itself in me, my psyche. As I stop below it and look up at the nerve endings of its branches, the tree reaches into me, my imagination, my historical memory, taking up space, flourishing. It's the maple beside our house in Bear River, Nova Scotia, when I was six, which I once fell out of. It's the skinny plaster tree Giacometti designed for Beckett's 1961 production of *Waiting for Godot*.

Perhaps you would see the tree you climbed with your first lover. Perhaps Dylan Thomas would have seen "The force that through the green fuse drives the flower." Perhaps Lorca would have seen a barren orange tree crying out to be freed "from the torment / of seeing [itself] without fruit."

In a flash, through the tree I see the root from which we all grow. An every-tree spiraling outward, linked to every living thing.

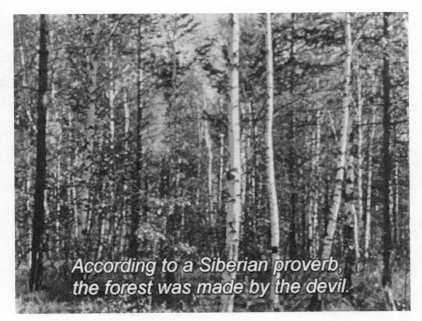

*According to a Siberian proverb,
the forest was made by the devil.*

Letter from Siberia (1957), by Chris Marker. These lines come next: "The devil did a good job; his forest is as big as the United States of America. But maybe the devil made the United States too."

Looking should be simple: there's an *eye* and a *thing*. My eye and the oak tree.

But as the world corrodes us, and our experience and trauma accumulate, looking becomes harder. We're quickly bored. On our way somewhere else, in a big hurry. We scan our surroundings for appeal, danger, utility. We move on.

It's easy, distracted as we are, to glance at a thing, but it's difficult to really absorb it. The absorption, I think, comes in two parts: the initial looking, and then sustaining that looking.

The initial looking can take a lifetime to foster. To learn to inhabit a space of calm and silence, within which we can be open to absorption. To unlearn what we've been taught about "beauty," "ugliness," and "pain." Then to become people who *value* beauty, ugliness, and pain.

Once we've practiced the first kind of looking, we can learn the second: developing a willingness to *keep* looking, even when we feel impatient and restless. Not looking away takes discipline.

Both kinds of looking are revelatory and transformative. To become a better poet, I want to nurture both. The work of all art, I think, is to relearn how we saw as young children: awestruck, absorbed.

To become image connoisseurs. Magpies. To see a shiny thing and collect it. Store it in our nest and make art with it later. In such a state of mind, the poem floods in.

I scoffed when I first heard Wordsworth's claim that he'd composed "Tintern Abbey" entirely in his head, in the carriage on his way home from the church ruins that day. I still doubt that all those lines of decasyllabic blank verse just came to him, ready-made. But I think it's possible that Wordsworth held his gaze on Tintern Abbey, looking deeply, and the form and spirit of the poem came to him in a flash.

The shiny thing I collected today is the oak tree. Later, at home, I reenact with language the reverie of my original seeing. This is what vision means for an artist, I think. If I succeed in transmitting that reverie, the reader can see the oak too. But if I don't, there's no amount of razzle-dazzle language, or playing with forms, that can revive my poem.

I'm learning, slowly, to see not just with my eyes, but also with fingers, nose, ears, tongue. To see with the mind, which is imagination. With feelings, memories, dreams. The hands, the heart. Reading, too, is a kind of seeing. Even talking.

Everything inside me, everything I am, brings me to the tree, to the moment of looking. The tree asks, What is inside you at this second? Anger, agitation, hunger? Or breath, heartbeat, focus?

What would the objects around us look like if we were centered, open? William Blake suggested, "If the doors of perception were cleansed every thing would appear to man as it is, Infinite. For man has closed himself up, till he sees all things thro' narrow chinks of his cavern."

I am dead sick of my cavern.

The tree sends me to my bookshelves, to movies, to Google. My curiosity, like lightning, branches in surprising directions.

I'm sitting in my living room beside a small stack of books of Japanese poetry. Haikus, I read, must contain a seasonal reference. I find a shiny poem by the seventeenth-century Japanese poet Matsuo Bashō: "The oak tree: / not interested / in cherry blossoms." That's my oak tree!

Bashō wrote in a simple, natural style, combining haiku, poetics, and his impressions of things he came across. He traveled alone, off the beaten path, on the "Five Highways" that connected Edo (now Tokyo) with the outer provinces during the Edo period (1603–1868). He was prepared to die on these dangerous roads, probably at the hands of bandits. His walks lasted years.

I find myself haunted by one particular passage in his book *The Narrow Road to the Deep North:*

> Go to the pine if you want to learn about the pine, or to the bamboo
> if you want to learn about the bamboo. And in doing so, you must

leave your subjective preoccupation with yourself. Otherwise you impose yourself on the object and do not learn. Your poetry issues of its own accord when you and the object have become one—when you have plunged deep enough into the object to see something like a hidden glimmering there. However well phrased your poetry may be, if your feeling is not natural—if the object and yourself are separate—then your poetry is not true poetry but merely your subjective counterfeit.

Instinctively I feel that this is where I've been heading. It's unclear to me from this translation of Japanese whether Bashō intended the word "glimmer," whose root comes from Old English *glæm,* "brightness." The spirit of Bashō's "hidden glimmering" might, it seems to me, be *scintilla:* from Latin, "spark, glimmer"; and figuratively: "particle of fire, spark, glittering speck, atom."

It's easy to imagine a "particle of fire" rising up out of my oak tree, as if formed by the friction and heat of my attention. The phrase "hidden glimmering"—more often translated as *underglimmer*—describes what happens in my mind when I have the patience to maintain concentration on the oak tree.

Bashō recommends that, while looking, we abandon our "subjective preoccupation" with ourselves: better to empty ourselves of expectations, rather than projecting our bias onto the object. Simply keep focus, he says, and the poem "issues of its own accord." With this looking comes a feeling of unity with the object, and with the world as a whole. When watcher and watched "have become one," the underglimmer comes to the fore.

For me, that's when language recedes and the object I'm looking at suddenly seems weirder. It's no longer an "oak tree," but an alien many-armed monolith; the dog is no longer "tan" or "Rottweiler," but a drooling comical thing of myth; the man is no longer "ugly" or "hairy," but pure energy, eyes blazing in midair.

It's in that place without language, I think, that the poem *sparks*. The release of the name of the thing feels almost palpable.

I think of it, the name, as a gate. Inspired by Bashō, I walk through this gate, into the unknown.

II. THE SECOND GATE

I find myself reading an old favorite, Anne Carson's *Short Talks,* and daydreaming about sneakers.

At sixteen, in 1985, I became fixated on the new Air Jordan 1 sneakers. It began with a worship of basketball god Michael Jordan, and jealousy of a fellow student who wore a pair to gym class. I made my father drive me all over Manhattan to find the exact color kicks (black and red) that Jordan wore on the poster on my wall: dunking the ball, tongue thrust out like a vengeful Māra demon. And finally the shoes were mine, out of the box, on my bed: clean, brand-new, dazzling.

In retrospect, I think my longing for the sneakers peaked before I owned them. My desire was not dependent on how they looked: though they were, I still think, impressive. I wanted the shoes because of what having them meant about me. I wanted a little flake of what Jordan had. The shoes spoke to my ego, my insecurities, my fantasies.

Bashō tells us that looking should not be a one-sided projection, a tyranny of the eye, as it was with me and my sneakers. Instead, looking should involve a kind of exchange between watcher and watched. Carson, in "Short Talk on the Mona Lisa," describes Leonardo da Vinci looking at his model, Lisa del Giocondo.

> Every day he poured his question into her,
> as you pour water from one vessel into an-

other, and it poured back. Don't tell me he
was painting his mother, lust, etc. There
is a moment when the water is not in one
vessel nor in the other—what a thirst it was,
and he supposed that when the canvas became completely empty he would stop. But
women are strong. She knew vessels, she
knew water, she knew mortal thirst.

Out of the deep silence of Leonardo, his utter absorption in Lisa's
face, comes the painting. But, in Carson's view, the model is an active
part of the process. There's communion: a pouring back and forth.
Is there desire? Perhaps, but also *recognition*. The scintilla rises between them, drifts back and forth, dynamic.

Looking at the oak tree, I feel this exchange. As if the tree had agency:
reaching inside me, scanning me like a text. In even the most jaded
of us, this feeling of connection can suggest some greater infrastructure, something bigger than ourselves.

And in this communion, this pouring back and forth between
watcher and watched, there is another palpable shift: desire falls
away. The second gate is desire.

In James Joyce's *A Portrait of the Artist as a Young Man,* the young
antihero Stephen Dedalus experiences such an internal shift. On
a walk by the Irish Sea, struggling with his guilt for visiting a sex
worker, mind full of fire-and-brimstone Catholic stories, he sees a
woman in the water:

> She seemed like one whom magic had changed into the likeness of a
> strange and beautiful seabird . . .

He turned away from her suddenly and set off across the strand. His cheeks were aflame; his body was aglow; his limbs were trembling . . .

. . . Her eyes had called him and his soul had leaped at the call. To live, to err, to fall, to triumph. . . . A wild angel had appeared to him . . . to throw open . . . the gates of all the ways of error and glory . . .

He felt above him the vast indifferent dome and the calm processes of the heavenly bodies; and the earth beneath him, the earth that had borne him, had taken him to her breast.

He closed his eyes in the languor of sleep. His eyelids trembled as if they felt the vast cyclic movement of the earth and her watchers, trembled as if they felt the strange light of some new world. His soul was swooning into some new world, fantastic, dim, uncertain as under sea, traversed by cloudy shapes and beings. A world, a glimmer or a flower?

Typical of Joyce, this section can be read in divergent ways. First, it describes Stephen the instant he becomes conscious of his power as an artist. For this, Joyce employs the language of ritual and myth: envisioning the woman as a "strange and beautiful seabird," half submerged in water, half reaching up to the stratosphere. Not a creature to be possessed. A language informed by the liminal "languor of sleep." A reverie. Evidence of Stephen's artistic revelation: an attainment of vision. The woman appears as a rite from deep in the earth, a "glimmer." The earth itself rises up in the form of a woman.

But, as we continue reading, we realize that the woman is probably urinating ("The first faint noise of gently moving water broke the silence, low and faint and whispering") and Stephen is probably masturbating ("to throw open before him in an instant of ecstasy the gates of all the ways of error and glory. On and on and on and on!"). The scene is more problematic than I'd assumed! Not free of desire at all. This doesn't fit into my essay as well because, at least on Stephen's part, it doesn't describe a Bashō-like relinquishing of "subjective preoccupation."

But, it's worth noting, there's a third way of looking at the scene: as not being either profane or holy, but somewhere in the middle. Certainly Stephen's gaze objectifies the woman. But if we read on, we see that the woman is looking back, too: "She was alone and still, gazing out to sea; and when she felt his presence and the worship of his eyes her eyes turned to him in quiet sufferance of his gaze, without shame or wantonness." The woman, far from passive, participates in the scene.

So is the passage transcendent artistic ecstasy, or smut? Can't it be both? Perhaps, for Stephen, desire—or its momentary suspension—is integral to artistic revelation. Perhaps his revelation is triggered by being watched in return, that communion, echoing the exchange between Leonardo and Lisa: "as you pour water from one vessel into an- / other, and it poured back."

Looking isn't pure. It's messy. Desire is messy. Vision is messy. The gates are *messy*. Everything about being human is messy.

The first gate, when the name falls away, is well-oiled, free-flowing. I'm used to looking at things and their names vanishing. But desire is a different story. This second gate, in my experience, is rusty, stuck, broken.

That said, sometimes, fleetingly, desire does evaporate while I'm in the process of looking. I'm in a mall holding the new Air Jordans, and suddenly they look weird, alien, fascinating. I'm connected to the sneakers, but how? I don't care what they give me, what they mean about me. In that moment I'm no longer a consumer, with what marketers call "buyer's eyes."

There is, in my experience, no complete relinquishing of desire. Just instants where desire is suspended. We pass through this second gate and return where we started in an eyeblink. Stephen's artistic revelation flashes by, and then his desire floods back. We can try to retain these moments, but the history of certain Catholic priests warns us of the dangers of forcing unenlightened abstinence.

There are moments when I look at the oak tree and don't want anything from it. When my bias and my ego seem to fall away. Lightning-bolt moments that I remember and carry to the poem.

For the magpie, such flashes are enough. The glittering world leaves us slightly dazzled, constantly.

III. THE THIRD GATE

A poet is the porous rag of the world, drenched and stained by everything they witness. Through their poem, we see with them, as they see. We are their proxy seers. The poet says, I have been looking. Here is my gold. "Anything you do not give freely and abundantly becomes lost to you," says Annie Dillard. "You open your safe and find ashes."

In the evening, still intoxicated by my contact with the oak tree, I watch two films by Chris Marker: *Letter from Siberia* (1957) and *Sans Soleil* (1983). Marker's films are documentaries, critical essays, nonfiction reflections, science fiction, photography, poetry, prophecy. Brimming with awe and wonder. Not reported information, but jewels held in cupped palms. Every frame personal, an offering, like the folded magazine articles (or photos or books or poems) my generous mother offers me every time I see her, which she's been dying to show me and only me.

Marker's films come from a zone of endless scintilla. Poem unlimited. Blinded by revelation. Visionary.

His films are full of looking, with the world looking back, like Leonardo and Lisa. *Letter from Siberia* looks at Russia. *Sans Soleil* looks at Japan and Guinea-Bissau and Hitchcock's *Vertigo*. With "obsessive curiosity," as Marker called it, he gathered images for years to make each film. One feels with Marker the sense of the artist as magpie, out in the world collecting bright things for us. In subways, markets, temples, bars, streets. The brokenhearted beauty of real folks. Their dream worlds. In *Sans Soleil,* as we watch images of taxidermied animals in sex poses, the voiceover tells us, "the Japanese secret—what Lévi-Strauss had called the poignancy of things—implied the faculty of communion with things, of entering into them, of being them for a moment." The scene shifts to Kiyomizu-dera Temple in Kyoto, a crowd of reverent people, clasped hands, downcast eyes, traditional Buddhist robes and beads. "There is a ceremony for brushes, for abacuses, and even for rusty needles. There's one on the 25th of September for the repose of the soul of broken dolls. The dolls are piled up in the temple of Kiyomitsu consecrated to Kannon—the goddess of compassion—and are burned in public."

Like Joyce, Marker loves how the sacred and profane mingle. Rusty needles, broken dolls. An animatronic JFK in a shopping mall. On a TV, wavering paintings of deer and this voiceover: "I've spent the day in front of my TV set—that memory box. I was in Nara with the sacred deers." Then a photo of a white bird in a tree, reflected in the river:

"I was taking a picture without knowing that in the 15th [*sic*] century Bashō had written: 'The willow sees the heron's image . . . upside down.'"

Marker transmits, somehow, a mindset we all recognize: deep attention. The mind quiet, present. Without worries, without plans. A mind I associate with making art. Being so immersed in a poem that if music is playing, I don't hear it.

Ironically, Marker's films are noisy. To make *Sans Soleil,* he captured documentary travel footage with a 16mm Beaulieu silent film camera and a non-sync tape recorder. (He swore he never knew what kind of films he was making until later, in the editing process.) He added sound after: voiceovers, recorded audio, music. The soundtrack— composed by him under the name Michel Krasna—is haunting: drone, ambient soundscapes, looped reverberations; it's unsettling, dissonant, and also, somehow, as absorbing as Tarkovsky's alien Zone in *Stalker,* which Marker refers to often. The zone Marker creates is both distinct and, as the title suggests, *sunless.*

They say that when you're watching a mainstream movie you shouldn't *hear* the music. Music's role is to foreground the action. If you do hear music, it has missed its mark; your mind has separated it from the action, and you're no longer immersed. Marker creates a noisescape in order to draw us into the broader cumulative effects of the film. Sound, in his films, urges us into a mental state of deep con- centration, like meditation. A reverie.

The third gate is noise. Walking through this gate, we enter silence.

I'm not a silent person. I struggle to sit still and listen. But the more I cultivate silence, the more it feels normal. I'm in an Uber looking out the window at an abandoned house, the word *"ENDLING"* spray- painted across the front door. Everything in my mind, everything I've done, everything I know, brings me to this moment of looking. A poem bursts out of the blue, as it did to Wordsworth in his carriage. In my Uber I whisper "Eureka!" as the Greek scholar Archimedes did when he discovered the principle of buoyancy in his bath and ran naked through the streets of Syracuse.

My mind, after an extended period of concentration, feels flexible, pliable, open. Clear, untethered. Silent.

It's our superpower, I think, as artists and humans. Attention is all we've got. My wife can feel my attention even if I say nothing. My cat, feeling it, reciprocates. This is how we show reverence, respect, affection. It's our strength, our only access to the deep song and to the supernatural. It's at the center of artmaking, meditation, prayer, and love.

Marker has found, in his singular film-essays, a form that holds many images, many ideas at once.

I've described what happens to my eye as I observe the oak tree. But the process of looking becomes very complicated quickly. First, no object is really still. Objects move. Buddhists and scientists agree that everything, however inanimate, is gravitating toward its own end.

Also, what happens when we look at two things, or at two hundred? Before our eyes, a child becomes a chaotic schoolyard; an anthill becomes a swarm; a city street becomes a mob. The thing blurs, abstracts. Morphs.

What happens when you try to hold an entire culture, or the whole world, in your mind? Ezra Pound—whose modernist collage-infused poetry in *The Cantos* surely inspired Sergei Eisenstein's influential film montages—showed that juxtaposed things create their own new relationship. Marker thrives in this distinct space, as he said in an interview, created "in the fashion of a musical composition, with recurrent themes, counterpoints, and mirrorlike fugues." His films relish montage, anachronism, synchronicity. The heat emerging from unlikely things—Japan and Guinea-Bissau, taxidermied animals and spiritual acolytes—rubbed together. In *Letter from Siberia,* a passing image becomes a central symbol of the film, a revelation about history and time:

In *Letter from Siberia,* the old world (four-wheel horse-drawn vehicle, called a telega) and the new (logging truck) cross paths.

And now here's the shot I've been waiting for, the shot you've all been waiting for, the shot no worthwhile film about a country in the process of transformation could possibly leave out: the contrast between the old and the new. On my right, the heavy duty truck: forty tons. On my left: the *telega,* two hundred forty pounds, the past and the future, tradition and progress, the Tiber and the Orontes, Philomena and Chloe. Take a good look because I won't show them to you again.

High afternoon sunshine on a dirt road, a river in the background. A truck hauling gigantic logs drifts right, revealing a horse and carriage drifting left. Somehow these unlike things, this anachronism, *fits.*

Marker's films hold unholdable things. Linking *everything*—countries, people, art, ideas, history—with holistic immediacy. He transposes two simple images, then adds more and more and more, for hours—weaving images the way, in *Heart of Darkness,* the three old women knit the threads of human destiny—forming a tapestry that enacts the entire world.

Slowly what has seemed *unlike* becomes *like*. Rivers from different countries, characters from different mythologies, are shown—as the noise rises—to be part of a single story. The past comes to us out of the present like a portent. Like a thought we already had.

In *Sans Soleil,* Marker drags us with him past the third gate, into silence. We feel that we are with him, beside him, in his visionary moment.

To achieve this degree of intimacy, he breaks every rule of film school: using bizarre angles, subjects staring into the camera, images out of focus or upside down. Anything to bring our attention to this instant, now, with him across time and space. Any innovation or "mistake" that *works* in this moment. Like Tarkovsky's Zone, the space *Sans Soleil* occupies morphs, disintegrates, reassembles, reinvents itself. A god's dream, free of categories.

We are looking at a woman. She looks away, shyly. We see, gradually, that she's aware of the camera. She allows herself, as Marker explains, a quick glance at us:

> My personal problem is more specific: how to film the ladies of Bissau? Apparently, the magical function of the eye was working against me there. It was in the marketplaces of Bissau and Cape Verde that I could stare at them again with equality: I see her, she saw me, she knows that I see her, she drops me her glance, but just at an angle where it is still possible to act as though it was not addressed to me, and at the end the real glance, straightforward, that lasted a twenty-fourth of a second, the length of a film frame.

I'm riveted, first, by the intimacy of this sequence, the electrical jolt of that one twenty-fourth of a second. The filmmaker is in love. And I am, too. But, as with Joyce and his "seabird" woman, it's complicated.

Sans Soleil (1983). The gaze returned, in Guinea-Bissau: 1/24th of a second.

In Marker's case, a white man looks at a Black woman in a country with a history of colonization by Portugal. Perhaps, one has to think, her version of this moment would have been different.

Was Marker, like Stephen Dedalus, ogling the woman? The exchange feels like affection, to me. But maybe that's what I want it to mean. In the end I don't know. The film, its context, its montage, reads me. It asks me what I'd like to take from this moment. It asks who I am. It allows me, in its silence, to create the scene myself.

That twenty-fourth of a second will strike you differently. Will light up different villages of your mind.

Watch it yourself.

IV. PAST THE GATES

The gates are mental markers we cross, consciously or unconsciously, when we keep focused on a thing. For me, at the first gate, the name "oak tree" falls away and the shape suddenly seems bizarre. At the second, I don't want the sneaker anymore, and feel that I could never possess it. At the third, my concentration on the abandoned house intensifies into a hushed reverie.

Looking deeply is difficult at first, I find, and then tremendously comforting. Since childhood I've been nervous, shaky; patience does not come easily. Years on social media—that oasis of fast gratification—have exacerbated my impatience. Before my focus expands, I wade through waves of restlessness.

But the more I visit this precious and rare space, the more my writing practice grows.

You might cross the three gates in a different order, at a different speed. But I trust that everyone recognizes the deepening of concentration that comes with crossing the three gates. It's the link between "hobbies," such as stamp collecting and checkers, and "high art," such as piano playing and oil painting. This muscle, which came to us naturally when we were kids, atrophies if we don't use it.

Since the space past the first gate is nonverbal, it's tempting to reach for grandiose language to describe what we see in there. As such, we use shorthand words like *perfect, essence, God, soul,* and *silence.* The language of faith and philosophy. Even Bashō, when he suggests that we "must" renounce "subjective preoccupation," might be reaching. Letting go of bias seems like a helpful suggestion rather than an ironclad necessity. As we look at an object, surely there will be some residue of who we are, our egos and personalities. Isn't it enough to *try* to let go of our prejudice, and let the object appear to us as it will?

Such hyperbolic language, while sometimes useful, can also be a trap. An excuse for us to stop looking and to sound clever in the process.

For as soon as we name the thing, or desire it, or stop being absorbed by it, we stop looking at it. Naming and possessing are illusory kinds of knowing, which provide a momentary balm because of course it's uncomfortable not to know. But ironically, when we think we know, we're as ignorant as ever, and robbed of the pleasures of looking.

The scintilla arises when I allow myself to look, to be absorbed, and not to know.

I stand, again, under the bare oak tree in The Woodlands. Despite my best effort to extricate my ego, as Bashō suggests, the tree still resembles the maple I fell out of in Bear River, Nova Scotia, 1976; and also the maple in my backyard in Halifax, 1982. I cast my soul out over the million trees I've seen, a blur of smells and touches and images and feelings.

The oak tree, my madeleine, triggers me.

When Bashō looks at the pine tree, he sees the poem. His own desire for the underglimmer. And perhaps his desire for us to see it, too.

When Louise Glück looks at a tree, in her poem "Copper Beech," she sees childhood. It reminds the speaker of a tree from her youth, when she was "a pointed finger." Through the tree, she sees back in time: a tree—of past, present, future—"rearing like an animal." Then come revelations about her parents: "one harsh, one invisible."

For Glück, as for us, literal looking—bringing attention to an object through our senses—is the initial trigger. Then comes the work of the poems and of our lives: concentrating, remembering, feeling, opening. As we pass through the gates, looking becomes figurative. And some glimmer always rises up. That's the gift of the world. We can't force the process but if we're patient, staving off aversion, every tree is an *axis mundi*.

In Alice Oswald's "Fox," the ear does the looking. The speaker wakes to a coughing sound: a real-world trigger that sets off the poem like a fuse. What comes after is all figurative, in the mind and heart of the speaker. She imagines a thievish fox in "black gloves" walking toward her in the grass. The ending is in the voice of the fox—who sees herself "laid beneath [her] children / like gold leaf"—but is, we trust, actually about the human speaker. A moment of reverence and devotion to her kin.

In Franz Wright's "September Sunflower," the speaker is convalescing in bed, looking at a sunflower. Although his ailment isn't clear, we know that Wright was hospitalized numerous times for substance abuse and manic-depressive episodes. As he stares at the "intense yellow flames" of the sunflower petals, an inward transformation takes place. As light floods the room, he thinks it's coming from the window, then realizes it's originating from somewhere else. Through the sunflower the speaker "loved again // And walked again."

Reading the poem, we experience a portion—a flake, a fragment—of the speaker's recovery.

What if we do *not* pass through the gates? What if we keep holding the name, embracing the desire, letting the noise in? Unabsorbed.

Many of us, me included, remain in this state most of our lives. Perceiving the world anxiously, nervously, hastily. Hoping for quick answers. In this mindset, I'm less likely to have the forbearance to outwait my first impressions. I project my preconceived ideas onto the thing, without experiencing the intense exchange or "mortal thirst" Carson describes.

When I write this way, my poems are drained, anemic. Written quickly. Read quickly, if at all. Forgotten.

But isn't this process (we gaze, glimmer rises), which I've described as a kind of magic, also naïve and possibly dangerous? Doesn't obsessiveness have a shadow side? Why do I assume that looking leads to positive outcomes?

When Hafiz looked at a rose, light emerged. But what about when Sylvia Plath "looked" at her dead father? Or when Hitler looked at a Star of David? When a stalker looks at a woman on a dark street, does a glimmer arise?

Not every looker is the same.

Sans Soleil. Woman on a ferry in Japan.

In *Sans Soleil,* out of nowhere, without preamble or voiceover, a giraffe is shot.

A male giraffe like a lighthouse in the desert. First he staggers on stick legs, blood spurting from his neck. A thread breaks and he falls back on himself. The ground rises to meet him. His neck unrolls like parchment, like a river. His massive body shudders, horribly, grasping for what is indestructible. Druidical knobs of his head in sand. His wound retches. He strains to stand, huge body in the dust. A man walks over, slow, shoots him in the head. Two vultures stroll into the frame, unhurried, feathered bankers. One pokes its beak deep in his eye, like a key.

How does light come from this? But it does.

In the objects around him, Lorca saw the torches and bullfighters of Andalusia. Mary Oliver, late in life, saw the dogs of Provincetown. Jack Gilbert saw the hot rocks of Santorini. Charles Olson saw the boats of Gloucester.

These are *their* images, the shiniest things they'd come across. Their idea of the sacred. Lenses through which they could see everything else.

My favorite kind of looking is compassionate. *Sans Soleil* is punctuated with prayer. Marker shows us minutes of prayer at a time, at various temples around Japan. He admires people's devotion, unironically.

On a train in Tokyo, face after face, nodding off, sleeping. Somnambulists. Gradually, lulling us into a reverie, Marker intersperses a montage of dreams, inner worlds: cartoons, eyeballs, naked bodies, a swordfight, shadows on the ceiling, sheets in the wind. "The train inhabited by sleeping people puts together all the fragments of dreams, makes a single film of them—the ultimate film."

And I realized that all of *Sans Soleil,* with its reverence and respect, has been prayer. And, maybe, Marker's entire life. And my entire life.

Because looking is prayer.

POSHLOST UNLIMITED

The chink in Chichikov's armor, that rusty chink emitting a faint but dreadful smell (a punctured can of conserved lobster tampered with and forgotten by some meddling fool in the pantry) is the organic aperture in the devil's armor. It is the essential stupidity of universal *poshlust*.
    —Vladimir Nabokov

I.

Poshlost (Пошлость), which has no exact equivalent in English, is a Russian word for a distinctly negative human character trait: banality, crudeness, sham. Snobbery, upward mobility, self-importance, lack of self-knowledge, social climbing. Google translates it as *vulgarity.*

The conceited, pompous, imperious butler in *Twelfth Night,* Malvolio, drips with *poshlost* as he preens in front of the noble Olivia in the silly yellow cross-gartered stockings that he thinks will win her over.

Nabokov, who dedicates eleven pages of his critical book *Nikolai Gogol* to the notion of *poshlost,* cites other famous literary examples: Polonius in *Hamlet;* Molly Bloom in *Ulysses;* Anna Karenina's husband Karenin. In *Strong Opinions,* Nabokov describes *poshlost* as "Corny trash, vulgar clichés, Philistinism in all its phases, imitations of imitations, bogus profundities, crude, moronic and dishonest pseudo-literature."

There are moments, I think, when a certain kind of enflamed satire transcends its context and emerges as more than the sum of its parts. Such satire—if it's developed with dexterity and energy—does the full loop: portraying humans first as vain and ridiculous, then as sublime. Because we viewers identify with those being portrayed, this almost-mystical "loop" occurs within us.

Longinus, in *On the Sublime* (first century C.E.), defined the slippery word as "excellence in language," the "expression of a great spirit," and the power to provoke "ecstasy" in readers.

Wordsworth wrote in his notebook (1811–12) that the sublime occurs when "the mind [attempts] to grasp at something towards which it can make approaches but which it is incapable of attaining." As if our minds were too base and earth-bound to hold such grandeur. But, Wordsworth thought, our spirits *can* hold it, at least momentarily. In "Tintern Abbey," he describes the effect of such *holding* on our psyches:

> Of aspect more sublime; that blessed mood,
> In which the burden of the mystery
> In which the heavy and weary weight
> Of all this unintelligible world,
> Is lightened.

Sometimes, I think, in certain inspired depictions of human stupidity and degradation, the ethos can suddenly shift, through a kind of artistic transubstantiation, into its opposite: the sublime.

Such depictions can, while telling us how ridiculous we are, provoke a *lightening*, or ecstasy, within us.

Gogol, to Nabokov, was the master of *poshlost*. Gogol's 1842 novel, *Dead Souls*, which he called an "epic poem in prose," is a caustic satire of Russian society. The story follows Pavel Ivanovich Chichikov, a chubby middle-aged gentleman without much money or many prospects, as he arrives in a small town and attempts to charm local officials and landowners into falling for a singular scam.

The scam involves a pun on the word "soul." In Russia, before 1861, landowners could own serfs to farm their land. The landowners could buy, sell, or mortgage the serfs; to count them, the word "soul" was used. In *Dead Souls*, Chichikov wants to buy dead serfs from landowners. It's all done on paper, as a transfer of names: the landowner, if she sells a dead serf, is relieved of a tax burden; Chichikov can then mortgage the dead serf to the state treasury and make a profit.

Chichikov reveals little about himself as he drifts from room to room, party to party, in an attempt to acquire "souls." The novel has a kind of circular structure, made up of disjointed episodes, often lapsing into absurdity. Chichikov visits people typical of Russian middle aristocracy of the time: squires, a widow, a bully. Each, especially Chichikov, seems flat, lacking any inner world.

And each, scrambling to gain something from Chichikov, reveals himself as a fool.

Nabokov begins his exegesis on *poshlost*—or *poshl*ust, as he calls it, punning on the social-climber connotation—with mock frustration, listing his attempts to find this "one pitiless word" in English dictionaries: "'cheap, sham, common, smutty, pink-and-blue, high falutin', in bad taste' . . . 'inferior, sorry, trashy, scurvy, tawdry, gimcrack' and others under 'cheapness.'" He then zeroes in on the undertone of artificial, fraudulent: "*poshlust* is not only the obviously trashy but also the falsely important, the falsely beautiful, the falsely clever, the falsely attractive."

He relishes the writing style Gogol uses to create the satirical world of nineteenth-century Russia, and in particular how Chichikov morphs before our eyes from a kind of Everyman into a "huge flesh-colored worm":

> The immense spherical *poshlyak* (singular of the word) Paul Chichikov eating the fig at the bottom of the milk which he drinks to mellow his throat, or dancing in his nightgown in the middle of the room while things on shelves rock in response to his Lacedaemonian jig (ending in his ecstatically hitting his chubby behind—his real face—with the pink heel of his bare foot, thus propelling himself into the true paradise of dead souls) these are visions which transcend the lesser varieties of *poshlust* discernible in humdrum provincial surroundings or in the petty iniquities of petty officials. But a *poshlyak* even of Chichikov's colossal dimensions inevitably has somewhere in him a hole, a chink through which you see the worm, the little shriveled fool that lies all huddled up in the depth of the *poshlust*-painted vacuum.

Through the ludicrous vision of Chichikov (hitting, for example, his chubby butt on his foot while dancing) we see "the little shriveled fool" which is, of course, not just Chichikov, but the whole human race, us readers included.

There's something heartening about hearing the truth, even if it reveals that we ourselves have been complicit in a lie.

We artists crave, to some degree, to expose our souls. While making art, the fog within us (slowly, excruciatingly) clears. For artist and viewer, art is always, at least in part, a process of self-discovery.

When I read Gogol, it's as if the camera turns to face me, and I am Chichikov. My weaknesses—my only-child self-absorption, petty jealousies, insecurities, desire to be praised—drift to the fore. As I slurp my many daily coffees and gobble chocolate muffins, *I am Chichikov* "eating the fig at the bottom of the milk which he drinks to mellow his throat."

I laugh, wince with recognition, then laugh again.

II.

French film director Jean Renoir was, like Gogol, a biting satirist of his contemporary society, and of humans in general. There's a scene in his 1939 film, *Rules of the Game,* which seems to reveal—with the audacity of an X-ray—the savage shame that percolates under the veneer of privilege.

The film follows a group of bourgeois acquaintances for a weekend at the country château of a marquis. During a dramatic performance one evening—including a pantomime and a slightly terrifying danse macabre—the host, Robert, looking dapper and tiny in a tuxedo, hops on stage and announces: "Dear friends, I have the pleasure of showing you my latest acquisition. It's the high point of my career as a collector of musical and mechanical instruments. I think you'll like it. I'll let you decide."

A hush in the room. The curtain is pulled aside to reveal a colossal birthday-cake-like calliope: a garish music box. Robert counts to three, light bulbs snap on. The crowd *Ohhs* and *Ahhs*. Robert shouts "Music!" and the contraption—called *Orchestrion,* as it's designed to replicate a full orchestra—groans to life with corny carnival music. Three ornate cherub figures with bland expressions shift their arms robotically.

Robert looks back and forth from the crowd to the music box.

Renoir's camera hovers on a painting of a naked nymph atop the calliope, framed by lights. Then comes a slow, gorgeous panning shot from right to left across the three cherubs, resting finally on Robert's face. He licks his lips, peering nervously to and fro, bursting with pride and embarrassment. He has a little obsequious smile. Sweating, he wipes his mouth with a cloth.

Rules of the Game (1939). Robert's dubious triumph: showing off his mechanical toy.

Now we realize this scene is about him: Robert's inner world. Robert who doesn't play instruments, but chooses instead to spend his wealth on inhuman, mechanized machines. His expression is awkward to look at; we've seen more than we should. He cares *too much* about his silly contraption, and now doubts his decision to share it with others.

This moment is intensely uncomfortable, and somehow ecstatic. I have watched it over and over. In this instant we learn, *somehow,* not just about Robert but about being human. How, with our fragile egos, we are complicit in the human race.

Renoir later said, "I think it's the best shot I've ever done in my life."

Nabokov's definition of *poshlost* is incisive but, I think, limited.

In *Strong Opinions,* his discussion of *poshlost* spills over into a broad condemnation of contemporary writing that he does not like, including work with an "overconcern with class or race" and "political allegories."

In fact, Nabokov himself was hard to pin down. He wrote in so many voices and used so many literary frameworks that it's hard to know who he was or what he *felt.*

Does *poshlost* live at the hinge between satire and sincerity? When satire is imbued with feeling, it seems to catch fire and become capable of transubstantiation, into the ecstasy Longinus and Wordsworth were after. But this can occur only when we step out from behind our veils, which Nabokov would not have been capable of.

In my own poetry, I don't want the Nabokovian protectedness. I want my poems open, compassionate. Risking tenderness.

○

À propos de Nice—a 1930 silent short documentary film directed by Jean Vigo, with cameraman Boris Kaufman—depicts life in Nice, France: the people, their routines, a carnival, and social inequities.

The film begins high above with aerial shots and moves quickly to street level, palm trees, waves crashing. With a kind of obsessive anthropological curiosity, Vigo observes the bourgeois tourists walking the boardwalk: self-important upper-class denizens, strolling past the casinos, a pageant of top hats and monocles, umbrellas, neckties, pointed beards.

Vigo uses many techniques to lampoon the bourgeoisie. Nabokov might not have agreed that this film contains *poshlost,* as it deals with issues of class, but I think of *À propos de Nice* as *poshlost* unlimited. Vigo intercuts between the fancy tourists and various animals: an ostrich, dogs, seagulls, a crocodile, a cat. He flashes from rich casinos to poor slums, using a fast-cutting editing technique so that images blur together. The tempo is sped up so everybody seems to be rushing, jogging, running, in a big hurry.

The cumulative effect is one of distance and irony. Vigo is winking at us, asking us what we think of this spectacle. We are not allowed to empathize with the tourists; they, like Chichikov and the fools around him, have no inner world. In every frame Vigo captures some ridiculous yet frail gesture: a woman smiling grotesquely, a man checking self-consciously over his shoulder. Their egos and snobbery and awkwardness and lack of dignity accumulate into a comical giddiness.

To portray the carnival in the second half, Vigo ramps up the speed and absurdity. We watch a parade with gigantic heads and costumes

À propos de Nice (1930). The giddy dancers sprayed with confetti.

and masks. A chubby lady on a float is hit in the face with flowers, over and over and over. Everywhere flowers are being handed or thrown back and forth. A dog is eating flowers. A group of flappers in high skirts, filmed from below, dance on a stand, like goddesses, confetti everywhere, too fast, too excited. Vigo intercuts from the dancing women to "serious" things: gravestone —> dancing flappers —> soldiers —> dancing flappers —> warship —> dancing flappers —> funeral procession —> dancing flappers —> soldier with medals on his chest —> dancing flappers.

The giddiness becomes too much. All the serious things I value in this life, the dignity of human beings, the dead, the animals, are over-whelmed by the dancing flappers kicking their legs, always kicking, laughing and kicking, too fast, not a care in the world.

III.

But in that giddiness we feel Vigo the human being, Vigo the Marxist devaluing the rich and elevating the poor. And in that feeling-connection between director and viewer, somehow, the film transcends its circumstances.

I want all of this in my poems. The human degradation, the sadness, the empathy, the connection. I tried to write, in my book *The Mean Game,* little farcical fables satirizing human greed. But I'm afraid they do not achieve the frenetic intensity of Vigo or Renoir. That *poshlost.*

Fascinatingly, I don't think poetry *can* achieve *poshlost.*

Certain media seem right for *poshlost.* TV and its late-night comics; plays like those of Aristophanes and Shakespeare; definitely films. But not so much poetry. Poetry *can* lampoon, criticize, attack, judge—but when it does, it seems to lose steam and not quite soar. What poetry does best is something else. Poems, I think, achieve the sublime through more sincere, "spiritual" modes.

Is it the didactic impulse that poems can't seem to hold? Lorca, who calls intellect "the foe of poetry," might say so. Aside from wit and humor, which poems can certainly convey, satire requires attack and judgment. Prominent examples of satirical poems seem, in my opinion, to be missing something. Does anyone outside of a classroom read Alexander Pope's dull and dated "The Rape of the Lock"? Dorothy Parker, the most famous satirist poet of the twentieth century, certainly isn't dull, but I don't think her poems soar. Philip Larkin's work has a scathing wit, but—like "Sunny Prestatyn," which begins by lampooning a girl on a calendar, until the poster is vandalized and finally replaced by *"Fight Cancer"*—quickly becomes weird, thorny, unclassifiable. Poets seem to be aiming at something different from, or beyond, humor, judgment, and teaching.

Perhaps satirical poems, while containing a certain power and truth, nevertheless fail because they don't leave enough room for silence. Implication, rather than explication, seem to work better in a poem. Louise Glück says, "I am attracted to ellipsis, to the unsaid, to suggestion, to eloquent, deliberate silence." Poetry, perhaps more than other art forms, needs to leave readers space to imagine and think for themselves.

Sharon Olds' poem "The Pope's Penis" pokes fun at the supreme pontiff, but doesn't tell us why. She describes, to comic effect, his manhood moving with him under his vestments during the day, and then at night becoming erect "in praise of God." Olds doesn't mention the child abuse of priests, or millennia of patriarchy, but just leads us to the conclusion that the pope, with all his pomp, is as human as the rest of us, and just as silly.

Two poems that mock William Carlos Williams—his self-serious Poetry Voice—work well as satire, I think. Mary Ruefle's "Red" ridicules the famous wheelbarrow poem, with its "fucking filthy" chickens. Kenneth Koch, in "Variations on a Theme by William Carlos Williams," makes fun of Williams' (equally famous) plums poem. The speaker—borrowing Williams' aw-shucks-I-stole-the-plums rationale—apologizes for chopping down a house: "I am sorry . . . it was morning . . . / and its wooden beams were so inviting."

Perhaps—of the examples I can think of—Williams himself, casting aside all his I-am-a-sensitive-doctor swagger in "Danse Russe," comes the closest to satire transubstantiated: that is, to *poshlost*. The poem presents us with a naked figure, presumably the poet himself, all the more grotesque for dancing in front of a mirror. As in Vigo's film, the ego is on full display for us to tease. The poem even mocks "poetic" language ("I am lonely, lonely") and imagery ("I admire my . . . shoulders, flanks, buttocks"). But Williams' purpose in "Danse Russe" seems to be to gently lampoon his own masculinity. The sense of attack and judgment are mild, and the sublime, while close, remains just out of reach.

In the end, none of these poems quite achieve the *poshlost* spirit. They satirize, with tongue in cheek, but don't contain the vitriol of Gogol or Vigo, or the intensity of Renoir.

Vigo's youthful, delighted energy, full of Marxist relish in exposing the foolish upper classes, transcends the subject matter and flips into its opposite: the sublime. *À propos de Nice* reflects and then elevates Nice, the French bourgeoisie, and any zeitgeist reference points, cumulating into a vision of humanity. The film helps us to see what human beings are in their existential core: our absurd plight, and how laughable we look grappling for the things we want.

The Bakhtin-esque carnival goers, the chattering bourgeois tourists, the inane dancers, *are me.* I can't help but take a hard look at my own pretensions and lack of kindness. It's the same way I felt one day while standing in a bank lineup in Kotwali Bazar, a market in Dharamsala, watching the street unfold beside me. A procession of poor folks in rags, donkeys, monkeys, dogs, and one ornately hand-painted fire truck. They looked, all at once, ridiculous, pathetic, tragic, funny. And there I was, awkward in the extreme, a tourist like a "huge flesh-colored worm."

Despite my reservations about Nabokov, I think he's dead right in assessing what *poshlost* can achieve: "that Gogolian gusto and wealth of weird detail which lift the whole thing to the level of a tremendous epic poem." Yes!

Hatred of human cruelty is the engine that drives these satirists. Their desire to see a better world. The *gusto* of their conviction— while reaching for "imitations of imitations," as Nabokov says—lifts the work to the sublime. Such art, rather than simply inviting us to relish people's stupidity and feel superior, makes us recognize our own complicity.

That recognition, thought savage, comes as a relief. As Wordsworth says, "the burden . . . / Is lightened."

IN THE COLD THEATER
OF THE POEM

This is how you live when you have a cold heart.
  —Louise Glück

I.

The coldest I've ever been was in Muonio—northern Finland, above
the Arctic Circle, near the Swedish border—winter 2009. I was just
getting to know Tiina, years before we got married. We stayed in a
cottage with two other couples. It took more than a day for the fire-
place to warm up the bitterly cold space. At night Tiina and I curled
up together under thick blankets in our little wooden room. She surprised me when she spoke out of her dream, her eyes flickering. "Ice
sailors," she said, "navigate an ice ship on the ice. The mountain took
away our ability to forget, so we must abandon it." At night I gently
withdrew from her arms, slipped my parka over my pajamas and,
there being no bathroom, stepped outside to urinate in the bright
dark, alone in the snow. Minus forty, no wind. It was so silent. Such
quiet contains its opposite. Shrillness, stifled. Sheer, mute. I could

feel my body temperature lowering. Alone in that cold, I'd surely die in an hour.

Certain art reminds me, distinctly, of being out there in the cold in Muonio, among the frozen birch trees and ice moon. Art that makes me shiver, uncovering my deeper beliefs: that I will die, that this body is not permanent, that I would like to change my life. Such art I consider *cold*.

The films of Stanley Kubrick contain impossibly eerie spaces, paranoiac compositions. In *The Shining* (1980), the lunatic protagonist, Jack, unravels in the labyrinthine Overlook Hotel, followed by the smoothly gliding Steadicam. Kubrick composes his shots coldly: using symmetry, static framing, distance. Think of the Steadicam drifting into the great hall where Jack types "All work and no play ..." over and over. Or the famous ending in the hedge maze: that dead still shot—held, agonizingly, ten seconds—on Jack's frozen grimace. Such shots are at once mundane and violent. Kubrick designed films the way he designed the architecture of the Overlook: as disorienting structures that don't quite add up, unsettling the audience. The "eye" that captures the scene is unblinking, objective, unsympathetic.

Quite a few artists make what I would call cold art. I love them all ferociously. The sculptures of Louise Bourgeois, those bronze spiders crawling out of an infinite sinkhole. The unleashed free jazz rage of Amiri Baraka. Samuel Beckett's grisly, trammeled, self-harming misanthropes. Eduardo C. Corral's deep song of the desert on the U.S.-Mexico border. The emaciated self-portraits of Egon Schiele, blood on his lips. William Basinski's haunting ambient drone compositions, each a tale of encroaching dread. García Lorca and his giggling blood-soaked goblin *duende.*

Such art has the ability to pierce the heart with its flying horn like a bull, to knock us off our rigid plinths.

I think of mindsets as *realms* we visit for a while. They feel so real! It's always a shock when they suddenly vanish.

The word "realm" (from old French, *reaume:* "kingdom") connotes myth, psychology, and physical location. Buddhists sometimes speak of realms, or *realming,* in the psychological sense. Khyentse Norbu, Tibetan lama and filmmaker: "Loosely, you can say when the perception comes more from aggression, you experience things in a hellish way. When your perception is filtered through attachment, grasping or miserliness, you experience the hungry ghost realm." We can, Khyentse Norbu explains, be trapped in a realm, like anger or grief, or we may pass through it to something else: "Actually we are talking about experiences that can come within the course of a day. It's not a different place."

Cold art has the potential to shatter the realms we hide in. Cold art cuts us, wounds us. Doesn't Kubrick make us "experience things in a hellish way"? Exactly what else is art good for, if it can't jar us out of our old patterns of thinking?

Art can rattle not just our personal identities, but also our social identities. In the spiderweb-like society that surrounds us, there are powerful industries in place—media, education, entertainment, finance, food, and so on—that reinforce the same overlapping values on us all. We believe we came up with our ideas ourselves, that my realm is mine alone, but because the messages of these industries are so consistent, so seamless, so ubiquitous, we share ways of thinking with almost everyone around us.

In corporate countries like America, we're encouraged to feel, among many other things (like righteous fury), a kind of toothless optimism. We're taught that we are most productive when our purchasing power is high: then we don't have time or energy to impede the government, military, police, or other power structures. We can best fit in, we learn, by working until we're flatlined, buying products incessantly, not voting, not protesting, and so on. By buying Amazon products, I can turn my house into a kind of showplace like those I've seen on Instagram. An enviable space where I can hide. Through products we acquire an illusion of protection, contentment, empty hope. We can't live in a society with universal health care, but we might, if we land an adequate job, get on an insurance plan. We can't live in a neighborhood without guns, but we can purchase a gun ourselves. We can't relinquish our debt, but we can obtain credit cards. Instead of contentment or happiness, we can feel toothless optimism.

One of the industries with the highest impact on our collective social identity is advertising, which teaches us that our agency comes from our buying power, that we have no inner worlds, that toothless optimism is the best strategy.

The mid-twentieth-century world of ads—the Lucky Strike cigarette campaigns of *Mad Men,* the glossy magazine ads John Berger critiqued in *Ways of Seeing*—has been superseded by the internet. Now trillion-dollar corporations like Google and Facebook use algorithms to design pop-ups and embedded ads targeted at us personally: advertisers pay to spam our social media feeds and internet searches with products based on our specific demographic, informed by our recent clicks. We believe we see through ads, but their effect on us— our social interactions, our love life, our language, our dreams—is profound. They appear innocuous, so we lazily assume that we're immune to their effects. But, while we might ignore many, ads have a collective, mosaic effect. "The triumph of advertising in the culture industry," as Theodor Adorno says, "is that consumers feel compelled to buy and use its products even though they see through them."

Ads are the most distilled, ubiquitous form of subjective expression of our age. Being-for-Other, for Adorno, is the state we find ourselves in after thoughtlessly modifying ourselves to adapt to our surroundings, thus impeding the possibility of an authentic Being-for-Self. Without knowing it, we have adopted the language and thinking and gestures of ads. We post flattering pictures of ourselves in the best possible light, with gleeful faces, like models in a soda commercial. Then we wait, as if lobotomized, for the "likes" to roll in.

Cumulatively, over our lives, the exposure to all these ads has a destructive effect on our psyches. Art, especially cold art, can counteract it.

I don't think anyone would call me cold. I wave to my neighbors. I'll stop to give a stranger directions. Uncomfortable silences make me cringe. I am one of the toothless optimists. Clinging to moments of comfort. Watching "Married at First Sight" on Netflix, scarfing microwave popcorn, distracting myself from the corrupt government and the new storms rolling over the east coast of the U.S. every year, which rattle the windows of our row home in West Philadelphia.

But, with art, I like to be surprised. There is a great pleasure in being cut and battered by art. One way that art—particularly *cold art,* I think—shakes us out of our toothless optimism, is by telling us the story of the brutality of life on earth, by showing us how close to animals we really are.

In the first act of *King Lear,* Lear—powerful as he is on paper—lives in a Kardashian-esque realm of Being-for-Other, acquiring his agency from the opinions of yes-people. He is sentimental, narcissistic, weak-minded. He imagines that, being a king, he can make the world fit his notion of it; he would like, for example, to make his daughters Goneril and Regan love him. But such a realm is, of course, dangerous and unsustainable. Over the first three acts, Lear's assets, his esteem, and his power are all taken from him. Then Edgar arrives dressed as Poor Tom. In this "mad" person, Lear envisions the breakdown of civilization, which ultimately shatters his realm. Lear's culture and manners and ego must be stripped from him before he can see a human being, himself included, as it is: "a poor, bare, forked animal."

This vision of humans as animals gives me the shivers. As we witness Lear's revelation, we too are shaken out of our realms. It's a continual shock to us that we, like Lear, can't change the world, that we must adjust to the world as it is. It's a brutal reality that most of us, in our comfort-seeking lives, would just as soon forget. What happens to Lear also happens to us when we watch Lear. We're proxies for Lear: in the storm on the cold heath, rain whipping against our faces. This is cold art.

J. M. Coetzee's books are unfriendly, cynical, cerebral. Cold. In *Life & Times of Michael K,* Michael K has no luck. He's a poor man with a cleft lip. Even his mother is repulsed by him. A cruel civil war has torn his country apart. Everywhere he turns, he's robbed, denied, rejected. His mother decides she must return to the idyllic farm of her youth. Michael accompanies her. She dies on the way. He makes it his quest to return to the farm. After many hardships he arrives, but nothing improves. Starving, he chases a goat and finally kills it in the muck:

> He had never cleaned an animal before. There was nothing to use but the penknife. He slit the belly and pushed his arm into the slit; he expected blood-heat but inside the goat encountered again the clammy wetness of marsh-mud. He wrenched and the organs came tumbling out at his feet, blue and purple and pink; he had to drag the carcass a distance away before he could continue. . . . His hands and sleeves were full of gore; there was no water nearby; he scoured himself with sand but was still followed by flies when he returned to the house.

Having cut the goat's belly with a penknife in desperation, Michael is covered in organs and muck. As we read, it's painful to see ourselves in Michael, "hands and sleeves . . . full of gore." Hopeless, stripped of dignity. It disturbs the realm we've been cozily curled up in.

Artists like Shakespeare and Coetzee and Kubrick don't appear to be concerned with compassion or empathy or any of the qualities I treasure in myself as a person.

Kubrick, in the spirit of Keats' negative capability, seems to erase himself from the process of creation. What comes through, instead of autobiography, is a brutal vision, or a psychic X-ray of a human being. Although Kubrick certainly had biases and used filmic techniques to spin his stories, in the end he gives me the impression of leaving the subject alone, in the cold, in front of the camera. The results are chilling and forceful. Think of the "droog" Alex in *A Clockwork Orange* (1971), the camera zooming in, slowly, patiently, on his choking face and watery blue eyes, before he jumps out the window.

If we knew the value of suffering," says Mary Ruefle, "we would ask for it."

A Clockwork Orange (1971). Alex triggered by Beethoven.

◯

Yes, but what is cold art? It's a short story whose main character I hate until suddenly I do not, and I find myself lowering the book and making a little sound at the back of my throat. It's an abstract painting that, even in a stiflingly muggy room, makes me shiver as in Muonio among the night birches. It's a film that appalls me but then later fragments of it float into my dream and I wake scribbling a poem about it into my notebook.

Cold art conveys a brutal "truth." But truth in art is, as Emily Dickinson tells us, *slant.* We'll never reach a consensus about what is true in art, or even what is good art and bad art. In a work of art, like a play, truth isn't determined by one scene or one mood or one character. But the aggregate of all the scenes and moods and characters together amounts to an impression. This impression may be thought of as cold or warm.

Most art is too slippery—shifting under our feet, chimeric—to categorize in such a binary way. Even a short poem, even a line, oscillates between cold and warm. A deft poem can evoke warmth just to shock us with coldness, or the other way around. The process is dynamic, inviting us to participate, if we choose to accept.

James Tate's later poems frequently shift back and forth from dead sober to wildly funny. In "The Cowboy," the speaker finds an alien in his kitchen. The alien loves John Ford movies and everything to do with cowboys. The alien asks for sarsaparilla. They become fast friends. The speaker offers to take the alien "to meet a real cowboy," in Wyoming or Montana. The end of the poem, which has thus far been spoken in a folksy vernacular, makes a cool shift when the alien reveals that it will soon die: "probably / my reward for coming here safely and meeting you." The cold finale, which is surprisingly touching, could not work if Tate hadn't shown us the warmly quirky camaraderie of the unlikely pair.

To be distinctive, coldness needs a counterpoint. The cold artist puts a cushy rug under our feet, then pulls it away. As we spend time with a work of art, our assumptions accumulate: we think the world is one way, but really it's another. We think the king is a fool. We think the alien is going to Wyoming. Then, amid the aggregate of scenes, comes an unexpected variation. A deviation. Overturning of expectation. Breakdown of cause and effect. As a result, our certainty is shattered. The self-control we cherish vanishes. And—sometimes, beautifully— the surprise of the poem is a revelation on the street.

There's a twin in the room. The tone familiar, strange. *Unheimlich.* Home and alien. There are two Jacks: the charismatic father overseeing the Overlook and the maniac creating a literal hell out of the hotel. Hope and despair, side by side. We, the audience, feel real hope for Jack the father. The hope builds in us as we watch him. Each time Jack speaks to his son, each time Michael K arrives in a new town, each time Lear meets his daughters Goneril and Regan, we think, *maybe this time it will work out for them.* As their lives worsen, as despair grows, still we cling to hope.

Cold art cannot exist without flashes of warmth. Where there's cold there's warmth. One implies the other. Cold art builds hope, thwarts it. This oscillation makes the work dynamic. Art without hope is a theater of cruelty. Marquis de Sade's *Juliette.* Tobe Hooper's *The Texas Chain Saw Massacre.* Michael Haneke's *Funny Games.* Cold without a smidge of warmth. Melancholy unlimited. Cormac McCarthy, in *Blood Meridian,* treads dangerously close to glacial nihilism, but allows in just enough warmth for a certain oscillation.

The oscillation happens within us, the viewers, in the theater of the mind. That's the feeling of lowering the book, making a small sound. Widening in our chairs.

II.

Warm art is not the opposite of cold art. It's not a zero-sum game.

Where cold art makes me shiver with the possibility of death, warm art makes me giggle with the possibility of pizza. Warm art is a friend you like to drink beer with, but you might not mention to them that you have cancer. Warm art forgot, at some point, that suffering exists. That struggle exists. Warm art tells us we're all right the way we are. Reminds us to put on our mittens. As if we had all the time in the world. As if suffering were not omnipresent. As if warm art himself were not suffering before our eyes. Warm art's intentions are clearly so good. What harm could there be?

Cold art is the friend you want to spend your last night on earth with. Cold art looks you square in the eye, speaks their truth.

"Do what you are going to do," says Sharon Olds, "and I will tell about it."

Warm art reaches too quickly for sentiment. Perhaps the artist, feeling a chilled panic, wants to assuage the viewer, or herself. This can happen even in a heartbreaking, beautifully crafted novel like Steinbeck's *Of Mice and Men*. Big, lumbering, "simple," doomed Lennie likes to pet his mouse with the tip of his finger. His best friend George tells him, "'That mouse ain't fresh, Lennie; and besides, you've broke it pettin' it. You get another mouse that's fresh and I'll let you keep it a little while.'" Here, with the dead mouse, Steinbeck has reached too willingly into the cookie jar of pathos, and the cold spell is broken.

In Clark Park, West Philadelphia, two blocks from my house, there stands a monument to warm art: a statue called "Dickens and Little Nell," by Francis Edwin Elwell. The stouthearted author sits on his majestic writing chair, while the young girl admires him from his ankles. The death of Little Nell, angelic preteen orphan-heroine of

Dickins' *The Old Curiosity Shop,* is one of the most famous episodes in British literature: "She was dead. Dear, gentle, patient, noble Nell was dead. Her little bird—a poor slight thing the pressure of a finger would have crushed—was stirring nimbly in its cage; and the strong heart of its child-mistress was mute and motionless for ever." Oscar Wilde responded, "One would have to have a heart of stone to read the death of little Nell without dissolving into tears ... of laughter."

Warm art—to borrow from the ancient Greek archery term *hamartia,* sometimes translated as *sin*—"misses the mark." But how? A surfeit of pity? Sweetness that just doesn't scratch the itch? Warm art, in the end, leaves us in our realm. Not to interrupt us. It's polite. *Romantic.* And, as Louise Glück says, "romance is what I most struggle to be free of."

According to Nabokov, even Dostoyevsky—whose novels are full of violence, addiction, and poverty—misses the mark: "Remember that when we speak of sentimentalists, among them Richardson, Rousseau, Dostoyevsky, we mean the nonartistic exaggeration of familiar emotions meant to provoke automatically traditional compassion in the reader." While *Crime and Punishment* is brutal at times, Nabokov argues that it leans too hard on romanticized notions of poverty and spiritual redemption: "Raskolnikov for some reason or other kills an old female pawnbroker and her sister. Justice in the shape of an inexorable police officer closes slowly in on him until in the end he is driven to a public confession, and through the love of a noble prostitute he is brought to a spiritual regeneration that did not seem as incredibly banal in 1866 when the book was written as it does now when noble prostitutes are apt to be received a little cynically by experienced readers."

Even when the topic is gravely important, and the artist is sincere and gifted, the result can miss the mark. In Steven Spielberg's Holocaust film, *Schindler's List* (1993), Oskar Schindler watches the Nazis' 1943 liquidation of the Kraków ghetto. Schindler is on a hill, on horseback. It's filmed in black and white. Wet, violent, chaotic. Machine guns rattle. A young girl in a red coat walks by, led by hand. It's the only color in the entire movie. We watch the girl in red run away past terrible vistas: Jewish folks shot in the head, corralled into trucks. She enters a house, hides under a bed, her hands over her ears. The film cuts back and forth from her to Schindler's horrified face, as if he were watching her the whole time, even under the bed. Later Schindler sees her body in a wagonload of corpses. This little girl, we understand, is Schindler's reason for saving so many Jewish people in his factory.

It's a very famous scene. Bring up *Schindler's List* in any crowd and someone is bound to mention the girl in the red coat. But it misses the mark, I think, because Spielberg overdoes it. First, by adding color. Second, by showing us the girl at angles Schindler could not possibly have seen. Spielberg—to help us *not miss her,* the significance of her—says, Feel for her *now.* Pay attention! But we were *already* paying attention. It's a cold scene, beautifully filmed. By forcing the feeling upon us, Spielberg lets our organic emotions slip away, and all that's left is sentiment.

Son of Saul (2015, dir. László Nemes, Hungarian) follows a Hungarian Jewish man for a day and a half in Auschwitz, 1944. Nemes lets the horrific scenes flow naturalistically, without telling the audience what to think about them. In Nemes' vision of the concentration camp, despite overwhelming despair, there is a sense of muted hope in the air which, partly because it's never overstated, does not turn sentimental.

Mirrors are cold.

I love the word "mimesis." It's derived from the Greek *mimeisthai,* meaning "to imitate," and is the root of *mime, mimic, imitation,* and *mimeograph*. Hamlet's famous advice to the players: "hold . . . the mirror up to nature."

Mimetic art is enactment: the playing out, or manifestation, of the thing itself. Demonstration rather than command; production rather than reproduction. But isn't art really a separate, *new* thing? Neither a copy of the thing nor the thing itself. Neither reflection nor absorption.

Nature doesn't favor angelic orphans, kindhearted oafs, noble sex workers, or girls in red coats. Nature has neither agenda nor mandate. R. H. Blyth's definition of sentimentality: "We are being sentimental when we give to a thing more tenderness than God gives to it."

The artist's truth is illusory. If the subject is a tree, the artist reflects it with not one but five, or six—or *fifty*—mirrors. And they're funhouse mirrors, of course, distorting the tree till it's unlike anything in nature.

One night in Muonio the six of us stood at the edge of the frozen lake and watched the northern lights high above. A green shimmering cloth, twisting slowly, endlessly, like a Möbius strip.

Can you almost feel the cold rising up out of the bright snow?

By cold art I don't mean cynical, unpleasant, or passionless art. Or art that seems to have been made by a hard-hearted, aloof human being. I'm not searching for the word "frigid." I certainly wouldn't go as far as Yvor Winters, who, in his poem "On Teaching the Young," suggests that poets seek "cold certitude— / Laurel, archaic, rude." I, for one, am not looking for "cold certitude." I appreciate artists puzzling through problems, not pretending to have answers.

I crave an obsessive focus on *the thing,* with minimal distractions. When the object feels embarrassingly close. Where it stops and we start is not sure. Artwork feels, in such moments, like "the thing itself"—as Lear describes Poor Tom—and not a facsimile. Transcending the artist, lifting the viewer.

Most Hollywood movies miss the mark, distracting us with action and effects, using simplified cues to evoke a Pavlovian response: sad character —> cue rain on window —> audience weeps. Such blatant manipulation might make us feel something in the moment, fleetingly. But when the lights come on, we forget every detail. As if it never happened.

Kubrick is subtle. In *The Shining,* Jack is seated on a barstool in the Gold Ballroom, wiping his hands on his face, deeply distracted, as if dreaming. He removes his hands, emerging from the dream, looks dead into the camera, *at us,* and says, "Hi, Lloyd. A little slow tonight, isn't it?" Lloyd—the bartender, part of the infernal dreamworld of

The Shining (1980). Jack chatting with Lloyd the bartender in the Gold Ballroom of the Overlook Hotel.

the hotel—is now a double for us, the audience. So Kubrick thrusts us into Jack's nightmare, and leaves us alone with him.

Think of two friends delivering the same terrible news. One is histrionic, gesticulating wildly, shouting. The other is impassive, providing the bare sketch of the news without affectation or interpretation. The histrionic friend, while perhaps catching us in their emotion, bullies us into feeling their way about the news; this removes our ability to process the news ourselves. The impassive friend has not tried to force us into thinking or feeling any particular way; and therefore, with our agency intact, we're free to respond according to the dictates of our hearts and minds.

Cold art is, of course, the impassive friend.

I enjoy many poets whose work I'd call warm. I love Billy Collins and Mary Oliver, for example, but I would not depend on them to tell me their whole truth. They prefer, perhaps, to please me, to wish me well, to enable me. There is a place for them on my shelves. After a hard day, tired in the evening, I will reach for them.

But they don't give me that shuddering thrill. They do not, like certain close friends of mine, stop me mid-sentence to challenge the bullshit I've been speaking. They do not lock eyes with me and tell me what's really on their minds. They will never change my life.

At times just a hair's breadth separates warm art from cold. John Haines' poem "Winter News" is as cold as hell in theme and tone but in the end reaches for warmth and, I think, comes up short.

The poem describes the ruthless cold near Fairbanks, Alaska, where the poet lived: freezing water wells, steam rising off the street, dying dogs. The images transport me to Muonio. Even the time of day, evening, conveys the sensation of life coming to an end. In the last stanza, a snowman calls "the white- / haired children home." I imagine the poet intended the snowman's voice to emanate in part from the children's mothers and in part from the great beyond—as if from the "mind of winter" itself, as Wallace Stevens calls it in his poem "The Snow Man." The voice Haines develops is eerie and effective. But the final word, "home," falls flat. As if Haines, seeking a familiar image to create a clear landing and oscillation in his poem, settled too quickly on a platitude and broke the spell.

III.

Trees of ice. A windless night. Nothing can survive out here for long.

The scene in the Muonio forest is embedded in my archetypal mind. The way my grandmother's apartment in Inwood, Manhattan, has become an every-apartment, infinitely malleable, in my imagination and dreams. So the Muonio forest is my deathbed. My last moments. When there's no further need to talk nonsense. All that's left is to speak from the heart with cold clarity.

One poet whose voice sounds, to me, as if it emerges directly out of that icy forest is Louise Glück.

Compare, for example, Glück's poem "The Drowned Children" to the Haines poem. Both describe children in a brutal landscape. In Glück's case, it's a cold pond that claims their lives. While Haines alludes to the kids' mortality, Glück's drowned children remain dead ("blind and weightless") throughout. The children, as in "Winter News," hear a voice calling them at the end: *come home, lost / in the waters, blue and permanent.* But, unlike Haines, Glück does not reach for solace on behalf of the children or the reader. Quite the opposite. She lets the scene remain exactly what it is: horrifying.

Glück's poem does oscillate from cold to warm, briefly, by implying, from the mention of a lamp and tablecloth, that the kids lived a life of domestic comfort before they drowned. Also the voice calling out to them—presumably that of their collective mothers—seems to miss them and love them. But the very last word, *"permanent,"* brings us back to cold reality.

In her many books of poems, Glück's voice conveys a sense of disciplined self-analysis, intense inner dialogue, determination to arrive at conclusions about the self. Her poems are psychological, almost narcissistic, but never sentimental or Being-for-Other. She does experiment with registers: *Meadowlands,* for example, is wryly funny. But, by and large, her poetic voice is that of the clear-eyed, stern village elder. The seer, unsmiling.

Reading her poems, a frisson runs through me, as if she were speaking to me directly out of her dream.

Glück's book *Ararat* shows her willingness to step out in front of the ghostly gliding Steadicam of her own gaze. She observes herself with uncanny clarity and coldness. In "Brown Circle," the speaker's mother asks her a terrible question: if she dislikes her parents so much, why did she decide to have her own family? The speaker, considering her son, doesn't respond. As a parent, she wanted to be a thoughtful gardener, caring for each flower. But, like her mother before her, she overexamined and scrutinized, not allowing the flower space to grow. Her desire to possess and control created damage. In the final devastating lines, she vows to change her life: "to forgive my mother, / now that I am helpless / to spare my son."

"Lamium"—from *The Wild Iris,* a connected sequence using voices of flowers, a poet-gardener, and God—is about one flower that lives a cold life, obsessed with light. Glück's flower-speaker begins with an icy *ars poetica:* she has "a cold heart," and lives in the shadows of giants. She, feeling the warmth of indirect light, craves more but concedes that we don't all need the same amount. Certain flowers, she says, can generate "our own light." The light she speaks of is, I think, the vital force in all living things. She'd like more light and warmth, but has come to terms with existence in the shade. The final lines—an attack on those who believe they exist to pursue truth, which includes things that are cold—sound austere, bitter. The flower is aloof, but emanates a warm solace, too: she's isolated but self-reliant. Aware that beauty, even the beauty of community, is fleeting, the flower takes comfort in her distant observations.

No wonder Charles Simic said that Glück "writes in an idiom that is as old as literature."

Muonio has become my personal metonym for the deep coldness at the base of life on earth. For the hard feelings we'd all prefer to ignore, like suffering, sorrow, depression, death.

Cold art, as it enacts the moment of dying over and over, isn't interested in death in itself, but wants to remind us of mortality. We are, as at a funeral, not the corpse but the mourners. The life force still surges within us. Cold art doesn't urge us toward nihilism, but reminds us to live now, to get things done, to be vital. This is the wisdom of it. Without such reminders we risk becoming fools, like Lear.

Cold art is not harmful or *bad* at all, but provides a useful counterpoint in our society to "happiness," which is severely overemphasized. Our existence naturally oscillates between warm and cold. This oscillation must be allowed, or the pendulum will break.

When the deep cold is invoked—in a poem, a song, a painting, a voice on the subway—the windless ice forest wakes within me. And it's in me always, the cold. The spiritual, psychic cold. While driving my motorcycle through the potholed streets of Philadelphia, chatting to my mother on the phone, watching a film, eating dinner with Tiina. That cold forest, its myriad frozen boughs, bristles within me.

In Muonio Tiina spoke out of her dream, using images from outside our window. And, just as I was falling in love with Tiina at that moment, I also fall in love a little with anyone who cares enough to tell me, speaking out of their dream, what is outside their window.

I crave this. I want my cage rattled. I want to be triggered. To lurch out of my realm. I want to be reminded. That something has gone gravely wrong with the human race. That people are trapped in huge, indifferent machines, fated to die alone, without any clear meaning or hope.

IV.

Light rises from the snow, absorbing the darkness in the air.

Your body temperature is lowering.

THE ENERGY CHARGE
(IN THIRTEEN PARTS)

1. Everyone is bored at the poetry reading. I am the most bored person at the poetry reading!

2. I wander the streets of West Philadelphia (to shake off the poetry reading!) reciting the poems of Warren C. Longmire. Listen to this: "I am not a fan of landscaping. I like armpit hair. I always show up undressed. My chest is full and blushed every sentence. I am the smallest possible dense, the ant, man and the dirt is where my riches lay."

3. The poem should be, has always been, a rage, a rush, a river bursting its banks. A rasping scream. William Blake knew. Listen to this: "Bring me my Bow of burning gold: / Bring me my Arrows of desire: / Bring me my Spear: O clouds unfold! / Bring me my Chariot of fire!"

4. Make my heart race so I'm embarrassed to feel so much on a park bench. Embarrassment is key. Be awkward in a poem. Never lie again in a poem. Share what is none of my business. TMI. Leave restraint at the school, the ceremony, the dinner table. Listen to Natalie Diaz: "I am in the dirt for you. / Your hips are quartz-light and dangerous, / two rose-horned rams ascending a soft desert wash / before the November sky untethers a hundred-year flood—"

5. Break your Instagram vows. Don't be polite for my sake. Make your loved ones angry. Anger is key. Over the fence from eloquence, brutality. Listen to Terrance Hayes: an "unarmed brother ground down / to gunpowder dirt can be inhaled / like a puff the magic bullet point / of transformation . . . "

6. We like drama and danger. We like movies. In the poem, too, something must happen. A poem is mammal, carnivore, leper, clown. Show us a poem slathered in blood and mud. Yours. Listen to Frank O'Hara: "My heart's aflutter! / I am standing in the bath tub / crying. Mother, mother / who am I? If he / will just come back once / and kiss me . . . "

7. In medias res, today, in sunlight, today, today. History now. Unfolding, as the mind unfolds, as dream unfolds. It's all we got. Without it we're fucked. Drag the dead across the border, to my house, now. Listen to Tranströmer: "And the God of the depths cries out of the depths / 'Deliver me! Deliver yourself!'"

8. Exhilarate me. And and and and and and bam. Change register. Let your pet lemur out to fight. And quietly. Listen to Adrienne Su: "Everywhere I go I meet anxious women / with money and beautiful faces, and men / with ashes on their brows. I'm lonely as hell." (Or or or or Natalie Shapero: "times I nearly died: careening / across Route 3 in the ice . . . / or seized by an undertow or by his hand.")

9. We are excited to be alive. Not human, necessarily. Just alive. How exhilarating, this improbable, momentary life. Listen to Jessamyn Birrer: "Abracadabra: The anus. The star at the base of the human / balloon. . . . / Crepe paper, the spiraling heart of the pipecleaner flower."

10. And the music of being alive.

11. There's energy in my surprise, surprise in my energy.

12. Leave little land mines all over the place. Let them tic tic tic a while, before dismantling them. Do not hurt anybody. Speak it all.

13. Until on the surface of your heart a crevasse or rift or *railo* which in Finnish means a crack in the ice and yes fall through.

THE MUSIC OF THE ZONE

The arena, the card-table, the magic circle, the temple, the stage, the screen, the tennis court, the court of justice, etc., are all in form and function playgrounds, i.e., forbidden spots, isolated, hedged round, hallowed, within which special rules obtain. All are temporary worlds within the ordinary world, dedicated to the performance of an act apart.
  —Johan Huizinga, *Homo Ludens: A Study of the Play-Element in Culture* (1938)

I.

The arena where a game happens, according to Dutch historian Johan Huizinga, is sacred. A closed microcosm where only the playing makes sense. The game, he says, "has no contact with any reality outside itself, and its performance is its own end."

As a kid in the late 1970s, in Halifax, Nova Scotia, I was obsessed with games. Toy soldiers, the Rubik's Cube, ColecoVision. I was a restless only child, by myself in my room, in the back seat of the car, absorbed in "temporary worlds within the ordinary world."

The Zone is a very complex maze of traps.

Stalker (1979). After just entering the Zone, Stalker, Writer, and Professor get their bearings.

Here I am in 1980, at ten, closing the door to my room, climbing the ladder to the wooden loft my dad built me. My bed up by the ceiling. Doubly private, very safe. Today I'm reading a Spider-Man comic. Other times I draw a picture, or just look down over my room and daydream.

Sounds drift in from the house: my mother preparing dinner, clinking pots and pans; the low drone of CBC Radio news; our dog, Alley, walking by, her nails clicking on the wood floors. Now I'm on my back, staring at the white ceiling, close enough to touch, the plaster I once gently cracked with my hand: a broken circle, mouth of a well.

At some point in my life, the loft transcended the physical space. In dreams the loft became a refuge where I hid from intruders. To this day when I read a book, certain fictional characters find themselves in my loft. It became an archetypal space. Hallowed, hedged round. A deeply personal, cordoned-off bed of the mind.

My parents still live in that house, but now my old loft stores blankets, towels, odds and ends. Below it, my dad sits at his computer playing online Scrabble. On visits I never go up there.

In my late teens I switched from playing games to writing poems. An easy transition because writing is a kind of game. Both involve puzzling through problems. Both require a mild obsessiveness: repeating an action over and over till it's right. Both demand child-like absorption, and *play*. And both occur in a play-space of the mind.

Now it's 2017, I'm forty-seven, living with Tiina in Dharamsala, Himachal Pradesh, India. I'm lucky enough to spend my days writing and reading. If I feel cooped up in my dark little spider-infested studio, I hike for an hour up to a plateau called Indru Naag which overlooks the Kangra Valley, the low misty hills of the Punjab in the distance. A serene spot—despite noisy paragliders drifting by, and Indian tourists at the nearby Hindu temple—to sit in the grass, read, and bask in the vista. I often bring a problem I'm puzzling over: a tricky unfinished poem, or a thorny idea. Each time, the walk and view have the miraculous effect of untangling the snarled ball of yarn that is my mind.

The long days in Dharamsala also afford me time to keep in touch with friends. Canadian poet Stephanie Bolster and I write back and forth so much that it's hard to know who came up with any particular idea. She sends her new poetry manuscript, which includes these lines:

When they enter the Zone there is colour.
This happened decades earlier.
When the house landed on the witch.
Her feet curled up. Water melted her green sister.
It's never easy in a place of colour.

The Zone she refers to is from *Stalker* (*Сталкер*, 1979), a film by Russian director Andrei Tarkovsky. Inspired by *Stalker*, Bolster and I had both written about zones. I send her my "Chernobyl" poem, in which Annie Edson Taylor, the first woman to go over Niagara Falls in a barrel, finds herself walking through a radioactive hospital in Pripyat. Bolster tells me about Robert Polidori's ruin porn photographs of Chernobyl and about Geoff Dyer, who wrote a book of essays about *Stalker* called *Zona*.

The Zone of *Stalker* becomes shorthand for us to talk about the forbidden spots of a poem. The space a poem takes up in the mind. The psychic landscape of a poem.

The plot of *Stalker* (loosely based on the 1972 science fiction novel, *Roadside Picnic,* by Russian authors Arkady and Boris Strugatsky, who also wrote the screenplay) is simple but elusive. A guide called Stalker leads two guests, Writer and Professor, into an enchanted area called the Zone. At the end they leave.

Opening credits inform us that the Zone was created by an alien visitation. "WE SENT THERE THE TROOPS IMMEDIATELY. THEY DID NOT COME BACK."

Few know of the existence of the Zone. It's encased in barbed wire, protected by military guards who fire machine guns at the three men as they break in. Inside the Zone there are no other people, but it's rife with life force. Wind heaves the high grass back and forth. Constant suffocating fog surges across the men. Pollen—is it *snow?*—swirls in the air. The landscape drips with *existence*. The visitors step with dread between predatory flora and rusted military machinery like megafauna skeletons in the grass.

The main character is the Zone itself. The three men are trespassers in the Zone and, we sometimes feel, in the film itself. They are always at risk of being rejected by the supernatural landscape.

Stalker warns his two guests to fear and respect the Zone: not to run or move unpredictably. Is it a minefield? "The Zone," Stalker says, "wants to be respected. Otherwise it will punish." How does it punish? Stalker doesn't say, but keeps tossing metal nuts tied to strips of cloth ahead of them, bracing himself for some retaliation.

Their destination is a wish-granting Room, which, we learn, has a dark side. A previous Stalker-guide named Porcupine led his brother to his death in the Zone, visited the Room, came into possession of a large sum of money, and then hanged himself.

Tarkovsky constructed his Zone to be deeply weird, utterly indescribable. A psychic landscape with unstable spatial properties. Its geography mutates, evolves, erased by fog, reborn by rain. Even Stalker, who's been there countless times, walks in circles, loses his way.

A spiraling metaphor, irreducible to language. The Zone reads us. Our minds; our thoughts; what we imagine possible. A political activist might see it as an allegory for a police state: a Cold War fantasy of bursting across a militarized frontier. As a poet, I think the Zone is the artistic process, how the artist enters a creative reverie: crossing the barbed wire frontier between normal life and a space of deepened focus.

As the three characters enter the Zone—painfully slowly, on a railway handcar—the bleak sepia landscape bleeds into a profound, almost psychedelic, green. Suddenly, as Bolster points out, there's color! Later they plod through a terrifying wet tunnel called "the meat grinder." Their destination, the Room, is both exhilarating and anticlimactic. Each of these stages can be thought of as mythic steps in the artmaking process: entering the trance, full immersion, and completion.

Stalker. Writer loses the bet (shortest matchstick) and must walk first through the deadly "meat grinder" to get to the wish-granting Room.

But is artmaking *dangerous?* Is art, as Stalker describes the Zone, "a very complicated system of traps"? For example, can the Zone be thought of as a metaphor for the life of Sylvia Plath? The caveat being, do not enter psychic terrain—that of others, or your own—without the obligatory fear and respect. In other words, using one's own psychic landscape as fodder for the artwork can traumatize, or trigger a psychosis in which one is unable to distinguish reverie from life, figurative from literal.

Stalker wears a constant expression of stunned paranoia. His wife pleads with him not to visit the Zone again. His daughter, Monkey, is disabled (unable to walk, or talk) and has telekinetic powers: all resulting from Stalker's trips to the Zone. A disquieting inheritance.

Consider, in Tarkovskian terms, the space of a poem. The poet enters the Zone of the poem, risking "punishment." The poet prepares the reader for the capricious Zone by surveying the property lines and marking the way to the gift-giving Room. So when the reader steps into the dense foliage of the poem, they shouldn't get lost or hurt. As such, poets are—at least upon the psychic minefields of the poems themselves—guides, or Stalkers, walking ahead of us, risking themselves so that we don't have to.

Tarkovsky has built a landscape outside time, outside narrative. The pacing crawls. He seems interested only in enacting the Zone, its ineffable powers, its unpredictability, its hazard. He will not entertain us.

The characters, as if to distract themselves from the menace around them, digress, babble, at times seemingly unconcerned by what they're talking about. Sometimes they just lie on the ground, as if defeated.

In *Stalker,* unspoken trumps spoken. For the viewer, paying attention to the quasi-philosophical, discursive conversations—as the subtitles, if like me you can't speak Russian, keep dragging our eyes away from the stunning cinematography—can be irksome. You want to tell the characters, "*Shhh.* Just look *around!*" For the land itself demands complete absorption. The four elements—spontaneous burning coals, wind gusting in trees, water gushing and dripping, earth pulsating, swallowed by fog—positively *throb.* The viewing experience entails, along with a certain fatigue and frustration, immersion in the Zone.

According to interviews with those on set, our agony as viewers might mirror the agony of creating the film. *Stalker* was filmed near Tallinn, Estonia, by the Jägala River. "Up the river," said sound recordist Vladimir Sharun, "was a chemical plant and it poured out poisonous liquids downstream. There is even this shot in *Stalker:* snow falling in the summer and white foam floating down the river. In fact it was some horrible poison."

> They botched the film or was it sabotage.
> Through the pipe of fear to where. They call it
> the meat grinder. A place of heaps of sand of saturation.
> Downstream from a chemical plant it seeped
> their deaths into them. They met it in reflections.
> You cannot go back the way you came.
> Next time will be different.
> —from "Shelter Object (Zone)," Stephanie Bolster

Some on the crew developed allergic reactions. Sharun goes so far as to blame the toxic location of *Stalker* for the early deaths by cancer of Tarkovsky, his wife Larissa, and actor Anatoly Solonitsyn, who played Writer.

In Russian, *зóна (zóna)* comes from the same root as the English word *zone:* from Latin *zona,* from Greek: *girdle, belt, to gird.* The Russian word connotes prison camp, or compound. The gulags—Russia's forced labor camps, ubiquitous in the '40s and '50s, in Tarkovsky's youth—used the same name: *зóна, zóna, zone.* Jägala concentration camp, a WWII German labor camp for Jews deported to Estonia, had been just down the Jägala River from the *Stalker* film set.

The contaminated area of Chernobyl, whose "catastrophic nuclear accident" occurred eight years after *Stalker* was filmed, is called "The Chernobyl Exclusion Zone": in Russian, *Зона отчуждения Чернобыльской АЭС,* or "The Chernobyl Nuclear Power Plant Zone of Alienation," or "The Zone of Absolute Exclusion."

Zone: "A definite region or area of the earth, or of any place or space, distinguished from adjacent regions by some special quality or condition." A literal or figurative arena "within which," as Huizinga defines a game, "special rules obtain."

There's an inside and an outside. Inside is the Zone, engirdled with barbed wire. Outside are "adjacent regions." It's not always possible, or advisable, to travel in and out of the Zone. You will need stamps, licenses, passports. Without them, guns will be fired at you.

The fences are high and the barbed wire sharp. If you spend too much time inside, you become alien to the outside. Aliens, of course, infected the Zone. An infection Stalker passed on to his "mutant" daughter, Monkey.

Monkey: a psychic, yet unable to walk. Half-mutant, half-goddess.

While inside the Zone, enjoying its special rules, it's easy to forget the outside. Stalker's nameless wife, considering her existence with a man compelled to enter and reenter the Zone, speaks directly into the camera: "It's better to have a bitter happiness than a gray, dull life." Bitterness, for her, is born in the Zone. But she'll stay with Stalker because it's better to have some happiness with the man she loves than "a gray, dull life" without him. She prefers—and who can blame her?—to live adjacently, contiguously. We all have our private, inviolable definitions of alienation.

A poem is an addictive landscape, like the deadly poppy field of Oz. A space closed off by the barbed wire of absorption. A continual present. The Zone of the poem requires the poet-Stalker and the reader-guest to remain, as much as humanly possible, in the delicious state of rapt immersion.

"It is so quiet out here," says Stalker; "it is the quietest place in the world."

"The Zone," says Geoff Dyer, "is film."

This is, first, literally true: Tarkovsky captured the landscape near the Jägala River on film stock, later chemically developing it into visible images that became the Zone.

Second, the Zone is what happens to us as we watch the *Stalker* film.

Nothing in the Zone is real. It's *imagination,* which is where inspiration comes from and where inspiration goes. We invent the Zone as we watch. When a black dog appears, trotting in the river, lying down next to Stalker, it's not an actual dog but an aspect of the Zone: a suggestion, a mirage, an archetype. This dog reminds us of all the dogs we've ever witnessed, including in pictures, and even in thought and dream. Containing the cumulative energy of our experience of dogs. In short, the black dog is a manifestation of the Zone: as hallucinatory and variable as everything else in that numinous space. Only at

The otherworldly dog appears out of nowhere and trots over to Stalker.

the end, outside the Zone, when we see the same black dog trotting beside Stalker and his family—with the Chernobyl-esque towers cooling in the distance—does the dog seem like a *real* thing that exists in time.

Tarkovsky preferred archetypes to symbols. Archetypes are ephemeral, energetic, freeplay. Symbols are expository, reductive, relying on a specific meaning or allegorical association. Symbols are heavier, harder to lift. The Zone is malleable, suggestive, direct, urgent—*à la* the black dog, or the immutable fog that negates all it touches like a thumb of God. The objects Stalker sees in the river—syringe, coins, religious artifacts—do not mean anything specific. We'd go mad trying to explain them. They mean what we think they mean in the glittering instant that we see them: just as a basketball might suddenly become a soccer ball or a doorstop, depending on who's playing or the time of day. Tarkovsky's archetypes are *film,* then nothing.

"The Zone," Tarkovsky once said, "doesn't exist. It's Stalker himself who invented his Zone."

Stalker opens on a sleeping family in bed: Stalker, his wife and daughter. A passing train shakes the house. "La Marseillaise," the French national anthem, plays faintly underneath that noise. "La Marseillaise" itself shakes the house. Then nothing, as if it hadn't played. Did we mishear? Are we in France?

When Stalker, Writer, and Professor depart the Zone at the end of the film, "Boléro" plays faintly underneath the rattle of a train. At the borders of the Zone, whispering at the edges, is classical music. A barbed wire fence of music. Are we now in Spain?

Within the Zone, sounds are distorted. As the trespassers first enter the Zone on a railway handcar, the repetitive noise of the wheels morphs into an electronic tone. Music, almost. Later, as the camera pans the rocks and moss of the visionary river, we hear Stalker's voice: "music, as if by some miracle, gets through to our heart." Music, like the omnipresent toxic pollen, emanates from the Zone.

As they step, slowly, carefully, through the Zone, there's a constant eerie soundscape of water: dripping, splashing, gurgling.

The Zone is water. A river, a mist, a rain. A human crying, bleeding. Spitting verse.

Poetry too emanates from the Zone, as if of its own accord. As the three lie by the river, sleeping, dreaming, a disembodied voice recites the Book of Revelation: colossal earthquake, sun turning "dark as sackcloth." In a huge hall with sand dunes, Stalker recites a poem by Porcupine's "sensitive, . . . gifted" brother (it's actually by the director's father, famous Russian poet and translator Arseny Tarkovsky), which is full of longing. The poem's speaker, after experiencing good fortune, warmth, light, keeps arriving at the same melancholic conclusion: "But it isn't enough."

II.

The Zone is a field of action.

William Carlos Williams' 1948 essay "The Poem as a Field of Action" is an attack on Eliot and Auden and sonnets and "the rigidity of the poetic foot," which Williams associated with British verse. He wanted a poem where the fresh, distinct American vernacular could have free reign.

Charles Olson's 1950 essay "Projective Verse" takes the notion of a poem as a dynamic space even further. With great bombast, Olson describes the urgent force of "composition by field":

It comes to this: the use of a man, by himself and thus by others, lies in how he conceives his relation to nature, that force to which he owes his somewhat small existence. If he sprawl, he shall find little to sing but himself, and shall sing, nature has such paradoxical ways, by way of artificial forms outside himself. But if he stays inside himself, if he is contained within his nature as he is participant in the larger force, he will be able to listen, and his hearing through himself will give him secrets objects share. And by an inverse law his shapes will make their own way. It is in this sense that the projective act, which is the artist's act in the larger field of objects, leads to dimensions larger than the man.

Tarkovsky would have liked this idea, that without "the larger force" of nature, the artist "shall find little to sing but himself." "What is it," Stalker asks, "that resonates in us in response to noise brought to harmony, making it the source of the greatest delight which stuns us and brings us together?"

Olson proclaims, "every element in an open poem . . . must be taken up as participants in the kinetic of the poem just as solidly as we are accustomed to take what we call the objects of reality." For Olson, Huizinga's field, with its "special rules," would be a poem: a kinetic space containing the "secrets objects share."

In *The Varieties of Religious Experience,* William James describes the soul "putting itself in a personal relation of contact with the mysterious power of which it feels the presence."

Stalker, awestruck, continually weeps.

Self-serious geniuses gesturing exaltedly can grow tiresome. Both Tarkovsky and Olson sometimes sound like they're delivering news from a mountaintop.

It makes me crave fresh voices, like that of Mary Ruefle, whose poems are sharp, nimble, playful, unruly. The opposite of arrogant. A Ruefle poem doubts itself, changes its mind. Best of all, she has a sense of humor.

Yet—like the work of Tarkovsky and Olson—Ruefle's poems exist in kinetic fields where, invigoratingly, anything can happen. In the countries where Ruefle is queen, citizens are amnesiacs, dreamers, sacred fools. Every poem is an opportunity to build and rebuild the ruined world with language. Trying to situate yourself in her poem "Timberland," for example, is as precarious as running in the Zone. Beginning in Paul's Fish Fry in Vermont, we suddenly find ourselves eating a juicy litchi in Guangzhou, China, then on a freight train barreling east out of the Blue Mountains of Oregon. The poem hurls us back and forth, keeping us unsteady, lightheaded. Soon as we find a foothold the speaker tells us, "Actually none of this has happened yet." All we can do, in the arena of Ruefle's poem, is submit to the noisy uncertainty of "the boxcar of a freight train / hurtling toward Pocatello, Idaho." All night she looks up at the stars, her head on the logs: "all / I can say is I am *happyhappyhappy* to be here."

Ruefle invites us to join her at the "un- // believable speed" of both the train she describes and the poem she gleefully conducts. The speaker's mother thinks she's in bed; her friends think she's on another train, which derailed. "But," she says, "I'm *here* . . . " Where, we ask, is that? Vermont, or perhaps China? Does it matter? We're in the poem, that ecosystem, which is exhilarating. To follow we must release. The shifting field of action demands our flexibility and complicity.

It feels as if Ruefle has created a Zone for me, personally. A space beyond time and logic, with a John Wall Barger–sized nook on a hurtling boxcar, open to the stars. I love being there, in Ruefle's poem. I visit it sometimes, or it visits me, while I'm falling asleep, or on a bus. The warm familiarity—combined with a certain Tarkovsky-esque hyperawareness—reminds me of when I was a kid in my loft.

After Stalker leaves the Zone and reunites with his family. Is that Chernobyl in the distance?

At the Indru Naag plateau, my bare feet in the grass, I read Tomas Tranströmer's poem "From the Thaw of 1966" to the glittering rooftops of the Kangra Valley:

> Headlong headlong waters; roaring; old hypnosis.
> The river swamps the car cemetery, glitters
> behind the masks.
> I hold tight to the bridge railing.
> The bridge: a big iron bird sailing past death.

In the Zone of Tranströmer's poem, *we* are on the bridge, water gushing beneath us.

He puts the items in place—roaring water, cars, bridge—like props of a theatrical production. Then he needs us readers to step onto that stage with full hearts.

So I do, at the Indru Naag plateau. All at once, impossibly, water surges, floods the grass where I sit. I am an amnesiac—all canons and tongues are mine—in the urgent, uncertain present. Soaked, clasping the railing, dizzy, exhilarated. Sailing out of my life.

Tranströmer's poem carries us, despite ourselves, to flashes of our own destruction. It passes quickly but when it's over, however shaky we remain, we are refreshed.

Comparing a bridge to a bird doesn't make sense: the bird isn't metal; the bridge can't fly. But what in the Zone does make sense? Its irrationality lodges itself in our minds, like so many moments in *Stalker*: the bird vanishing midflight, the uncanny dog, and of course the daughter—so-called "victim of the Zone"—sliding glasses across the kitchen table with her mind.

The engine of the Zone is metaphor. In the Zone objects morph, contort, glitter. Quicksilver, fairy dust. *Radiation.*

III.

The Zone of the poem is made up of the combined sentience of poet and reader. The poet infuses the Zone with their whole psyche, then departs. That Zone then requires the psyche of the reader to resuscitate it.

"The room of desires," Tarkovsky explained, "is ... yet another provocation in the face of the material world. This provocation, formed in Stalker's mind, corresponds to an act of faith."

A poem is a provocation because it inhabits a surrogate space "dedicated to the performance of an act apart," whose rules resist nature.

A poem is an act of faith because the poet believes in it, though its ecosystem is held together only by the gossamer scaffolding of words. The poet must, further, have faith that guests will visit that ecosystem and partake in the performance.

For that performance to work, the rules of the ecosystem cannot be too rigid, logical, or grammatical. The guest of the poem must be invited, with tact, to participate.

Readers should be drawn in by the play of mad drummers. Once in, there should be oceans for the readers to map, binoculars to peer through, animals to name.

If the poet scribbles the word "stone" on every stone, and leaves the price tag on every dress, the reader will—like Porcupine and his brother—simply vanish. The reader loves to touch objects with wonder. The reader loves to step off path into the brambles where it is shadowy and prickly.

When the poet invites the reader, with tact, and the reader enters, with wonder—oh, it's an uncommon and lovely communion. Two psyches constructing the space together, outside of time, in harmony, as if under the stars in a boxcar, "*happyhappyhappy*." A kind of shamanism.

The poem, as Huizinga said of the play-sphere, is only concerned with its own reality. Like the "magic circle" of games and digital media (where "normal" reality is suspended and replaced by the artificial reality of a game world), the poem refers only to the poem. Words point to words, fashioning their own logic as they are spoken. I enter your Zone, my psyche porous. I accept what I find and repurpose every object in real time to make it my own. In such a space the reader has unheard-of powers. Time travel, flying bridges, vanishing birds. Piece of cake!

Tranströmer: "I am not empty, I am open."

I believed Stalker was the poet. He's not. He's God, walking across the field of himself.

I believed the Zone was inside the artist. But it's not inside or outside. It's both inside and outside.

There is nowhere that is not the Zone.

Sit in the writing chair. All your things around you: books, lamps, blankets. Dishes clinking, low drone of a radio, dog clicking by in the hall.

Block it out. All of it. *Now* you can start.

Climb the high fence, always in your chair. Your pants tear on the barbed wire, you fall hard on the grass on the other side.

Now there's color. Green, how I want you green. Who said that? Never mind. What pleasure to let such green soak your skin. Everything's wet: the field, the river, the house. *You* are *soaked*.

Walk the field. It hums, a low drone of . . . bees?

The river is weird. Hard to see. Was the house so tall? Whose black dog is beside you? That humming, is it the river?

Step into the house. Into the Room. Sit on the floor. The hardwood, crosslegged. Shut your eyes. Can you feel how it—the house, the field, the river—all of it, exists without you? How it doesn't need you? You're helpless. The music is louder.

Breathe, eyes shut. Vertiginous, uncomfortable. Familiar.

On October 24, 1901, on her sixty-third birthday, Annie Edson Taylor went over Niagara Falls in a barrel.

The barrel, custom-made out of oak and iron, padded with a mattress, included Taylor's lucky heart-shaped pillow. As she climbed in, her friends held the barrel steady in the water. She blew them a kiss, they shouted *Hoo-rah!* and sealed her in by screwing on the lid, compressing the air with a bicycle tire pump, and plugging the hole with a cork. They urged the barrel adrift. The tiny ark.

Shut your eyes, darling, against the dark. Breathe, relinquish it all. The craft begins to rock.

Roaring toward an unseeable edge.

THE AMNESIAC AT DUSK

Have patience with everything that remains unsolved in your heart . . . live in the question.
  —Rilke, *Letters to a Young Poet*

I. BREAKING

At twenty-nine, in 1999, I had a mental breakdown. After living for two years in Europe, I returned to Halifax, to my parents' house where I'd grown up. My five-year marriage had blown apart in Italy. Depressed and overwhelmed, I'd planned to visit Halifax briefly and then to travel with my remaining savings to India. My parents, watching me as if I were a curious animal, suggested I stay with them in Halifax for a few months to rest.

I'd written, *dabbled,* since I was a teenager. I knew I wanted to be an artist, and craved a deeper connection to art. I'd tried poetry, fiction, painting, playwriting, even acting. I'd done, of course, a lot of living: marriage (no kids); graduate work (English lit); tree planting (North

Mountain, Nova Scotia); waiting tables (Dublin); English teaching in Ottawa, Rome, and Prague.

I eventually found that connection through poetry. The turbulent period in 1999 was the fertile ground into which my poetry life was planted.

It began with my mother, Jean. Agreeing to rest rather than travel to India, I lived for a few months in an upstairs apartment in my parents' house. In that close proximity, Jean—a vegetarian, meditator, and overall creative and gentle person—put me on a healthy regimen. She taught me yoga, enrolled me in a meditation class. She bought me a copy of Julia Cameron's *The Artist's Way* book, which provides week by week exercises and notes for "stuck" artists. One of the exercises is morning pages (writing three pages quickly when you wake up), which Jean and I both did each day.

Jean suggested that, rather than wallowing, I could help others, so I volunteered to teach in a literacy program at the public library. She also said I should do what I enjoy, find my bliss, if it's not harmful or addictive. After struggling to articulate what that could be, I finally came up with one blissful thing: *dusk*. I'd always enjoyed dusk. So I decided, every day I'd walk at dusk.

And I did. For one year, each day—no matter where, with whom, how busy, in what weather—I walked for a few blocks while the sun was going down. For those few minutes of dusk, no matter how miserable and exhausted I felt, I let my mind and body wander where it needed to go, in a space tinged with positivity and kindness. It was a start.

Serendipity: "the faculty of making happy and unexpected discoveries by accident." The positive connotation of "luck" or "good fortune" became popular in the twentieth century.

In 1922, microbiologist Alexander Fleming sneezed into a Petri dish full of bacteria, which led, they say, to his discovery of penicillin. "Nature makes penicillin," Fleming said, "I just found it; one sometimes finds what one is not looking for."

Serendipity is related to coincidence, lateral thinking, and Jung's concept of synchronicity: "the phenomenon of events which coincide in time and appear meaningfully related but have no discoverable causal connection." In his book *Synchronicity* (1960), Jung describes a patient who was relating her dream to him, about a golden scarab. As Jung explains it, at that moment "a gentle tapping" came at the window: it was a scarabaeid beetle, "nearest analogy to a golden scarab that one finds in our latitudes."

Horace Walpole—best known for *The Castle of Otranto* (1764), considered the first Gothic novel—discovered the word "serendipity" by accident when he came across a copy of a 1557 Persian book called *The Three Princes of Serendip.* The tales in it were ancient, probably from India, since *Serendip*—from Sanskrit *Simhaladvīpa:* "Dwelling-Place-of-Lions Island"—is the Persian name for Ceylon (modern Sri Lanka).

On January 28, 1754, Walpole coined the word "serendipity" in a letter to Horace Mann, calling the Persian book a "silly fairy tale" about three princes who "were always making discoveries, by accidents and sagacity, of things they were not in quest of."

It feels good to know things. To feel sure. We base our identity and happiness on what we know. *"Scientia potentia est,"* as Sir Francis Bacon said. *Knowledge is power.*

We know that the sun will rise, that we have (or do not have) a job, that we have (or do not have) a certain amount of money in the bank, that we own (or do not own) a working car, that our society is (or is not) economically stable, that we are (or are not) at war.

But, of course, none of these things are stable. They are all changing constantly. Even the sun!

In Buddhism, the first noble truth is that all life is suffering *(Dukkha)*. The second noble truth is *the cause* of suffering *(Tanhā)*: that is, craving, desire, attachment. These, Buddha said, are two things we can know.

We are attached to our conceptual apparatus: the idea of knowledge, the idea of a self, the idea of separation between things in the world. These concepts undergird our many expectations.

In *Zen Mind, Beginner's Mind,* Shunryu Suzuki says, "If your mind is empty, it is always ready for anything, it is open to everything. In the beginner's mind there are many possibilities, but in the expert's mind there are few."

II. ZEMBLANITY

Memento (2000, dir. Christopher Nolan) is about an amnesiac, Leonard Shelby, who's trying to solve a mystery: who killed his wife? Since he suffers memory loss every few minutes, he must constantly think on his feet, using the tattoos on his body and the Polaroid photos in his pockets, with notes on the back, as clues.

Shelby exists in a constant state of hyperawareness and fear, seeking signs and signals as if his life depended on it. His amnesia—full of psychic pain, disorientation, panic, horror—is not the kind of empty mind Suzuki was referring to.

Wandering the city in agony, pushing against the not-knowing, Shelby is a walking embodiment of Heraclitus' dictum: "The unlike is joined together, and from differences results the most beautiful harmony, and all things take place by strife."

After that return from Europe in 1999, I was surprised by how devastated I felt. After all, I'd *wanted* to end the marriage. I'd wanted to return to Canada. Nothing catastrophic had happened.

Nevertheless, I fell into a two-year-long spiral of depression. Every day crept slowly, painfully. What did I have in the world? What should I do? I took solace in ephemeral pleasures, like sex and recreational drugs, unsure of who I was in my core.

Holding strife close, the old notions of self. Not letting go. Numb. I seemed to remember, dimly, a sense of inspiration in the past. Far away.

My dusk walks were joyless at first. Putting one foot in front of the other in the pink light. I knew it was a good idea, that I could trust my mother's advice, but wasn't sure why. What should I be looking for? What would I find?

William Boyd, in his novel *Armadillo* (1998), coined the term *zemblanity* to mean the opposite of serendipity: "making unhappy, unlucky and expected discoveries occurring by design." A *zemblanity,* Boyd says, is a kind of "unpleasant unsurprise." He borrowed the term from an Arctic archipelago in northern Russia: Novaya Zemlya. In the sixteenth century, Dutch explorer Willem Barents and his crew were stranded on Novaya Zemlya while searching for a new route to the east. It's a cold, barren land with many features opposite to those of lush Sri Lanka (i.e., *Serendip*).

That sense—I felt it every day for two years, and still feel it sometimes—of *trying* to be open, to find inspiration, but instead there's only the cold islands of *zemblanity.*

In the Argentinian film *The Headless Woman* (*La mujer sin cabeza,* 2008, dir. Lucrecia Martel), Verónica, a middle-aged dentist from a wealthy family, has a car accident and believes that she has run over and killed a little boy.

In the accident, Verónica hits her head on the steering wheel. The camera holds a medium close-up shot of her profile. Beside her, on the window, the handprints of a child. Verónica looks at them. Are they from the boy she might have hit, or the boys in a parking lot in the previous scene? For the rest of the film, Verónica wanders around in a concussed, semiconscious, *lost* state. Heartbroken, guilt-ridden. Following traces of what happened, only half-realizing where she is and who she's talking to.

Martel makes us feel that we, the film's viewers, have experienced Verónica's accident, and what comes after, first-hand. Camera shots

Verónica, in *The Headless Woman* (2008), moments after her car accident. How can we stop looking at the uncanny handprints?

are disorienting. Action occurs in Verónica's peripheral vision. Voices emanate from off-screen. We're not sure what we're looking at.

Throughout, Martel's camera hovers myopically close to Verónica's tortured face.

III. SERENDIPITY

As I walked in the dusk each evening, an intangible good feeling began *very, very slowly* to expand. To pool and drip into the other parts of my day. My existence, my search, had meaning somehow. An open feeling.

I had been struggling to know what had happened in my marriage, what job I would do, who I was in this new context. I'd been searching—desperately grasping, like Shelby and Verónica—for traces and answers.

I still felt this struggle, but also a shift toward something more active, positive. Away from the joyless hunt for knowledge, and toward negative capability: that is, "being in uncertainties, mysteries, doubts, without any irritable reaching after fact and reason."

Away from the concussed amnesiac, clasping his strife, that *zemblanity*. Toward the Aeolian Harp, which, according to the Romantic poets, wind passes through to make a song.

I began, at this time, to write poems more seriously. I started by simply underlining the "gold" in my morning pages and copying those lines onto another page. With this simple act, I had the foundation of a poem every day, which felt satisfying.

I once heard the sculptor Richard Serra say, "In order to make art today we need to have made art yesterday." That is, as artists we must be working all the time. Jotting down notes to return to later. Then we're already *inside* the work, at least partly inspired. In this state of mind, serendipity can play a role in our artistic process. Like Fleming and Jung, we can be open to the links between the things around us, and use our artwork to perform those links.

At the heart of my notion of serendipity is the trust that there is an infrastructure—call it God, dharma, karma, or nature—that connects our inner world to the outer world. To many, this might seem irrational. Schopenhauer, speculating on the transcendental, seems to imply that such connectedness is solely subjective: "All the events in a man's life would accordingly stand in two fundamentally different kinds of connection: firstly, in the objective, causal connection of the natural process; secondly, in a subjective connection which exists only in relation to the individual who experiences it, and which is thus as subjective as his own dreams."

Is the inner world really linked to the outer, by some invisible fibrous net? As poets, thank God, we don't have to answer such questions. In any case, like amnesiacs, we do find ourselves compulsively seeking lines, trails, traces between unlike things. That's what a metaphor is: an "illogical" association of unlike images. Pablo Neruda, for example, compares horses to fire: "Like waves of fire, they flared forward / and to my eyes filled the whole world, / empty till then" ("Horses"). Suddenly, on a bleak winter day in Berlin, the speaker sees within the horses a light he's been lacking. A kind of lasso joining the outer world to the inner.

What fascinates me as a poet is the feeling I get when I'm inspired, that intuitive sense that the substructure of existence somehow lines up. That there is a great pattern out there which I can see in fleeting glimpses. That seems true, but I couldn't say how. Writing poems, for me, means entering a mindset where I'm looking for clues, traces, *something*. Open to the swirling universe around me.

We often dramatize forgetting as painful, which it certainly can be. But memory is also a heavy weight to carry. We must, I think, sometimes let go of the knotty, burdensome apparatus that comes with life on earth. To make art, we need to walk around like newborns for a small portion of the day. Let ourselves *not know*.

If we're open this way, it's easier to find, as Fleming said, something we're not looking for.

James Tate's poem "It Happens Like This" enacts a space of awestruck openness.

As the poem unfolds, its ontology shifts. We think it's one kind of space, then it's another. The speaker is surprised to come across a goat in his small town. He walks away, the goat follows. He's bemused. Someone asks if the goat is his; he responds, no. Another asks if they can have a turn caring for the goat. The speaker says, "Soon.... Your time is coming." Suddenly he seems to know all about the goat and who should care for him.

When a police officer shows up, the speaker seems to know even more about the goat. He tells the officer that the goat's family has always lived in the town. We must now ask ourselves, has the speaker always known the goat? The further the poem goes on, the better the speaker knows the goat, and the deeper the mystery. The officer asks the goat's name, and if he can touch the goat. The goat's name, says the speaker, is the Prince of Peace. The officer gushes with unexpected self-awareness: "I'm just a child playing cops and robbers / forever. Please forgive me if I cry." The speaker forgives him and says, "we understand why you, more than / anybody, should never touch the Prince." The goat has transformed, before our eyes, into something sacred, Christ-like. But *how?*

Charles Simic says, of Tate, "To write a poem out of nothing at all is Tate's genius."

In 1999, rather than self-destructing, I—thanks to my mother's gentle nudging—became "addicted" to a certain kind of poetic wandering and serendipitous questing. By urging myself, in this turbulent period, toward fertile uncertainty and away from bleak *zemblanity,* I felt better. And I suddenly knew that poetry would be my life's work!

The poems I'm drawn to accept uncertainty. Rather than pushing against not-knowing, they allow it.

They're not trying to walk their way back to a preconceived answer. Each answer, in the space the poem creates, is as good as the next.

The amnesiac at dusk is, for me, the best mindset for writing a poem. For any act of creation, in fact. And all acts of creation, and the acceptance that comes with them, are tinged with the sacred. Through the work the artist is reborn, again and again, to the world and its sorcery.

Like Neruda's speaker, psychically reborn when confronted by the beauty of the horses. Or like Tate's cop, full of awe and gratefulness. Or like William Blake when, at age eight in 1765, he saw, in Peckham Rye Park in London, "a tree filled with angels, bright angelic wings bespangling every bough like stars."

Being human, of course, is not always the same as writing a poem. Life is thorny, tangled. It's hard, while being an Aeolian Harp, to operate one's smartphone or to catch a bus. But I think we can be inspired artists and also keep our eyes open to the complexities around us. Awe is not denial.

Since there is—increasingly, it sometimes feels—so much strife and pain in the world, this transmission of reverence, our contagious amnesiac feeling, is vital.

CLUB SILENCIO

]
]
deep sound
]

    −Sappho (Fragment 29A), trans. Anne Carson

I.

After a good day of writing, it's like I've emerged out of a dream. I can't remember where I've been or what I've written. As if rain had washed away my footprints.

I climb out of my red chair, eat a bowl of cereal, drink a coffee. I go for a walk around Clark Park. Later, returning to the writing, it's like stairs appearing in the mist. Stairs that lead from the literal space of West Philadelphia back into the grotesque, figurative landscape of the imagination. I spend my life moving between, at the edges of, these two spaces.

Jack Gilbert, in his poem "Beyond Pleasure," describes how writing can lead us back, step by step, to an experience outside the boundaries of everyday life.

> Gradually we realize what is felt is not so important
> (however lovely or cruel) as what the feeling contains.
> Not what happens to us in childhood, but what was
> inside what happened. Ken Kesey sitting in the woods,
> beyond his fence of whitewashed motorcycles, said when
> he was writing on acid he was not writing about it.
> He used what he wrote as blazes to find his way back
> to what he knew then.

Having taken a powerful hallucinogen, Kesey—the famous beatnik author of *One Flew Over the Cuckoo's Nest*—finds himself in a space beyond language. When he sobers up, he won't remember what happened. He might recall details, but the language will be different.

What's true of Kesey is true of all artists, stoned or sober. Our artwork acts as blazes that lead us across a threshold, from conscious to unconscious, from thought to feeling, from "real life" to the deepest cave of ourselves. Gilbert's poem, which describes Kesey going through this process, encourages us to do it ourselves.

Threshold-crossing. That precarious border. Like Orpheus, or Lot's wife, we should not look back. Just go where you are going, without hesitation. Then, for God's sake, come back.

Gilbert, later in the poem, claims that the best poetry "searches / out what is beyond pleasure, is outside process." Such poetry leaves markers along the overgrown trails that lead us *inward,* into our own dark hearts. Ariadne knew this. According to Hesiod, Ariadne fell in love with Theseus and gave him a ball of thread so he could find his way back out of the maze after fighting the Minotaur. Theseus was the hero, but Ariadne was the artist. She knew the cave, the dark that exists "outside process." She'd used the thread before, to find the middle of the maze. And, crucially, to return intact.

But some accounts say that Ariadne died by suicide. So perhaps she did not, in fact, return from all that threshold-crossing unscathed?

LIMEN

Threshold: A piece of wood, stone, or other material forming the bottom of a doorway, crossed as we enter a house, building, or room; the sill of a doorway. Old English *prescold:* "door-sill, point of entering."

A threshold, in other words, is a doorway separating where the family eats and sleeps from where they do work. Work, for certain farmers, meant threshing: separating the grain of a cereal crop from the husks and straw, the seed from the chaff, by shaking, trampling, and beating. Such work would have been done in a threshing area, near the house.

Symbolically, a threshold—this doorway separating inside from outside—indicates a possible transformation. We cross the doorsill, take a left out of our parents' house, toward the bus station; then, minutes or years later, we return. But the true threshold is within the house; we cross from inside to deeper inside. To a box under some photographs; to an unmarked file in a family member's computer. Into the pocket of the person sitting beside you at dinner.

We cross back and forth, all day long, from a conscious space (*room*) through a threshold (*limen*) into an unconscious space (*inner room*).

ROOM

The *room* is where we live our days: our mental state when we wake up, take the bus, go to the bank, make plans, socialize. The realm of language, articulation, performance, time. The not-dream.

The *inner room* is inside the inside of the house: a space of secrets, reverie, deep song, trance. The inarticulate, unconscious, subconscious. When we see a bird dying and *feel* something. When we dream or daydream. When we're immersed in work or lust or play, and we lose time. Think of an M. C. Escher house within a house. Or Kafka's court offices in *The Trial*. So many spiraling rooms, so few windows. A basement: location of horror movies, like *Nightmare on Elm Street*. And of real-life horrors: John Wayne Gacy buried dozens of teenage boys under the floorboards of his house in Norwood Park Township, a suburb of Chicago.

In the *Paradiso,* Dante envisions the Virgin Mary as a flaming brightness: "while smiling down upon their sports and songs / a Beauty I beheld, who was the joy / within the eyes of all the other Saints. / And even if I in utterance were as rich / as in imagination, I'd not dare / attempt to tell the least of its delight" (Canto 31, trans. Courtney Langdon). He can approximate her beauty, but ultimately admits that it's beyond language.

"The highest levels of consciousness," Charles Simic says, "are wordless."

The *inner room*—although ineffable, sacred even—is common, not precious. It's that feeling when we read a book and are immersed in an alternate world. All day—as we climb in and out of cars, sing a song in the shower, watch a film—we drift back and forth from *room* to *inner room*. From, as Gilbert says, "what happens to us in childhood" to "what was / inside what happened."

Kesey knew during his hallucinatory reverie that he was having an experience which would not transfer back to his rational mind, or *room*. He—lucid enough, apparently, to hold a pen—wrote down his mind-altering knowledge so that later, in his *room,* the realm of language, he might remember. The blazes—which "He used . . . to find his way back / to what he knew then"—are markers leading him, gradually, back across the *limen* into the *inner room*.

In my metaphor, we're lost in our own home. A disorienting, nightmarish notion. Perhaps—rather than burning the house down with blazes—Hansel-and-Gretel-like breadcrumbs would suffice to find our way from room to room.

LIMEN

The *limen* (Latin: "threshold, cross-piece, sill," related to *liminal*) separates *room* from *inner room*. A transition moment, a flash, a blink; a psychic door-sill, stairwell, Haruki Murakami portal, Tarkovsky tunnel. In the *Poetic Edda,* it's the Yggdrasil tree that Ratatoskr the squirrel climbs up and down, carrying messages between worlds. In *Ringu,* it's the well the vengeful spirit climbs out of. In *Beowulf,* it's the lake the hero dives into to fight Grendel's mother.

ROOM

David Lynch's *Mulholland Drive* (2001) is a kind of reboot of *The Wizard of Oz* (1939). Like *Oz, Mulholland Drive* takes place primarily in a dream space, in the mind of one of the characters. Lynch's ending, like the ending of *Oz* (Dorothy, back in Kansas: "But it wasn't a dream. It was a place. And *you* and *you* and *you*—and *you* were there"), articulates the protagonist's real-life connection to the dream.

Kansas is the *room*. When Dorothy's house is caught in the twister, swirling through the air, that's the *limen*. The witch and her monkeys, the poppy field, the Munchkins, the glittering kingdom of Oz, are all the *inner room*.

In the back-in-Kansas nondream *room* of *Mulholland Drive*—which, unlike in *Oz,* Lynch only reveals to us briefly at the end, implying that everything to that point has been a dream, or *inner room*—the protagonist, Diane, is a heartbroken woman torn apart by guilt because she hired a hitman to murder her ex, Camilla.

INNER ROOM

In the dream, Betty (Diane in real life) rescues an amnesiac named Rita (Camilla in real life). The two women search, Nancy Drew-style, for clues to Rita's identity. Toward the end, Betty and Rita enter what feels like the center of the maze, or a gate of hell: a theater called Club Silencio.

They watch a performance, a mind-blowing sleight of hand which reminds us why we love Lynch as a director. A goateed magician, in front of tall crimson curtains, pulls sound out of the air while telling the audience, "It's all recorded." A woman sings Roy Orbison's "Crying" in Spanish, heartbreakingly; she faints, her singing continues. We don't believe it's been a recording. It isn't! It emanates from *nowhere;* from the air, which is *film.* Betty and Rita recoil, weep.

Mulholland Drive (2001). Betty and Rita submerged deep inside Lynch's sublime vision of hell: Club Silencio.

Diane might be lucid dreaming in Club Silencio, her downward spiral finally bubbling forth into her waking mind. While listening to "Crying," she (i.e., "Betty") convulses, choking on tears. As if she's suddenly realized what she'd done: murdered the woman next to her, whom she loves.

After the performance in Club Silencio, the film shifts abruptly to "Kansas," the nondream. Diane is a struggling actress, rejected by Camilla. She has Camilla killed and shoots herself.

The film ends back at the theater with a blue-haired lady in a box seat whispering, "*Silencio.*"

LIMEN

Lynch's films, by thrusting us into the surreal without warning, blur the line between *room* and *inner room.* As with Blake, Stein, Buñuel, Borges, Murakami, and countless others, dream and reality intersect constantly. These are not mind states with clearly marked borders, but twinkling gates all around us.

Lynch enjoys constant ontological instability, indicated through "weirdness" like stilted dialogue. In fact, for Lynch, *limina* are ubiquitous. Everywhere we look are red curtains or fog or a flickering lamp or a rusted stairwell to indicate that a character is crossing from one psychic space into another. In *Mulholland Drive,* from a "normal" scene of two friends eating in a booth at a diner called Winkie's (*room*), we cross a parking lot toward an ominous dumpster (*limen*) where a nightmarish figure lurks (*inner room*).

Like the poems of Jack Gilbert, Lynch's films are lined with blazes leading the viewer inward. If we follow the clues implicit in his impossible performances, we find our way into the very middle of ourselves.

Winkie's diner, *Mulholland Drive*. Crossing the threshold, step by step: 1. Dan talks about his nightmare; 2. Dan investigates dumpster; 3. Dan's nightmare pops out; 4. Dan passes out.

II.

As we write poems we pause on the *limen,* as on the median of a busy street. On one side of us, where poems come from; on the other, where poems go.

Setting a poem down in language is a constantly unbearable process, because the *thing* that came to us originally—feeling, inspiration, impulse—never remains intact. The end result is always (I'll speak for myself) a disappointment.

To me, a good poem is not a reported description of a real-world thing. It's an approximation, using words (*room*) to describe non-words (*inner room*). T. S. Eliot, in his 1919 essay "Hamlet and His Problems," famously named this approximation: "The only way of expressing emotion in the form of art is by finding an 'objective correlative'; in other words, a set of objects, a situation, a chain of events which shall be the formula of that particular emotion; such that when the external facts, which must terminate in sensory experience, are given, the emotion is immediately evoked."

So, for example, I see a dog limping in traffic, cars swerving around it, and feel an emotion: a pang. With that pang, which happens in my *inner room,* comes the idea of a poem, a hazy inarticulate wisp of a poem. When I jot the word "pang" into my notebook, it materializes in the *room.* Passing through the *limen,* the image transforms, distorts. Specifically, the pang I felt while watching a dog in traffic ended up—significantly altered, many drafts later—in an actual poem of mine called "How to Float": "I mean, why don't we / drown every time we see a photo / of an elephant, face hacked off / by poachers?"

The objective correlative for my *pang* ended up being an elephant. It's a messy process, dragging precious objects back and forth across the *limen.* Very imprecise. Like slathering an angel with mud.

But there's also a kind of sorcery in it. A metamorphosis.

That's why I value poems that admit an incapacity to name. Donika Kelly's *The Renunciations,* addressing familial abuse, asks: "Did Daddy [   ]?" Such a poem, rather than articulating directly, acts as an arrow pointing within us as readers: an invitation to follow the blazes into our own murky psyches.

As Mary Ruefle says, "The great lunacy of most lyric poems is that they attempt to use words to convey what cannot be put into words."

Many of us, uncomfortable with approximating, oversimplify poems: making them literal, expository, newsworthy, inspirational, confessional. A great poem can be these things, within limits. I admit I prefer stubborn, weird, unwieldy poems that won't be told what they are. Such poems speak their minds of their own volition, I think. Or they *can* do so, if we who write them trust the very intuitive process that comes from spending time, a lifetime, on that *limen* bridge between outside and inside.

Rilke, in his poem "Pont Du Carrousel," describes such a bridge:

> The blind man on the bridge,
> gray monument to a fallen world,
> —he could be *it,* the thing we need,
> the one silent man, the hub,
> as the stars in their hours turn around him,
> as the city twirls and flaunts and struts around him.
>
> He's the just man, imperturbable
> in the terrible city;
> dark aperture to the underworld
> in a superficial age.

Perhaps the gray blind man is Louis Petitot's statue ("Industry," 1846) on the titular Paris bridge: a giant, "imperturbable" seated figure, above the gyring traffic. The statue, with its winged hat, resembles Mercury, god of messages (and travelers, boundaries, luck, trickery, thieves), who guided souls to the underworld.

Or perhaps the figure on the bridge is a poet. Standing—listening, uncertain, separate—at a cosmic intersection between worlds.

Motionless, hushed. Like Keats, at dusk, outside Fanny Brawne's house. Poem in his pocket. Message-bearer.

Yes, poetry misses the mark—always!—but that's part of its power. Poetry never quite captures what it tries to refer to. *Pang* is never "pang." The poem, a thing of language, is permanently severed from the dream where it originated. Umbilicus cut.

If a poet accepts that a poem is just language, this awareness—like Neo's awareness in *The Matrix* (1999) that the Matrix is an operating system and *not real,* so while he's inside it he has the powers of a god—allows the poem to be deliciously free from the logical constraints of the "real" world. A poem can be impossible, limitless. Free to follow rhythm or sound or metaphor down whatever rabbit hole opens up in front of it.

Jacques Derrida argued that there's no center, or presence, to language, and therefore nothing to keep the limitless "play of substitutions" at bay. There's never, he thought, a reducible signified, or transcendental meaning, that cannot be continually divided or displaced. This means that between words and objects is an irreconcilable disconnect, and this play of *"différance"* is the meaning we receive from language. Language, uncentered, is subject to manifold variations: *freeplay.*

But are words and objects *really* irreconcilable? Does language (such as a poem) really refer *only* to language?

Derrida's freeplay seems to describe a kind of nihilism—or Tower-of-Babel gibberish—where our thoughts constantly slide off of the words, with no clear reference to the world of objects. I like this idea, in part. But to me, language's disconnect from the real world feels partial, not complete. We search through language for traces of the world, trapped as we are between signifier and signified. Not entirely lost, or found. "The world is not a prison house," E. A. Robinson says, "but a kind of spiritual kindergarten, where millions of bewildered infants are trying to spell God with the wrong blocks."

We who live on the *limen,* that middle space, are the living tissue between dream and flesh.

Poems attain liftoff when their language lets go of its compulsive desire to refer to the real world. When poems revel in the play of substitutions, they find their frenzied radiance. It's the slippery, not-quite-earth-logic feeling of being inside a John Ashbery poem: "No sighs like Russian music, only a vast unravelling / Out toward the junctions and to the darkness beyond / To these bare fields, built at today's expense" ("Pyrography").

The middle space is a reverie. We're on the bridge between dream and waking. With access to both worlds. On the dream side, we see images sliding off each other, and hear gobbledygook words. On the waking side, we see solid forms, and hear words with solid referents. Lynch's movies occupy the middle space: Diane is sitting next to Camilla who is both dead and not dead. Poetic metaphors also exist in that space: Neruda simultaneously sees both "waves of fire" and horses.

This between-space might be nihilism but feels like freedom!

Poems abandon conventional reality and embrace freeplay to point to what I think of as a deeper reality. Zen Buddhism has helpful language for broaching this spiritual terrain: a Zen practitioner sits in silence to experience the deep truth of existence, or the world as it truly is. This, Dōgen said, is No-Self. Paradoxically, our truest self is No-Self, or emptiness.

I'm drawn to that liminal poetic space because I can intuit something underneath language that I want to be in contact with. It feels more real.

What I think of as freeplay—the dream-dance of signifier and signified in the *inner room*—is not nihilism but nondualism. It's the language of myth and poems, which sees the world as chimeric, shimmying, shifting. The irrational language of Zen koans. It's the sense that the objects around us are too big and unwieldy to be held by language, too shimmering and strange. Too *empty*.

The Heart Sutra says, "Form is emptiness, emptiness is form." While poems don't exactly offer us No-Self, they point to it by drawing attention to the ephemerality of existence.

If we're meditating, or absorbed in a poem, or in the dark watching a movie, or asleep, we have access to a world of forms that approximates my idea of how the fluid, interconnected cosmos actually moves, and how it's actually made up.

The truest approximation of myself is silence.

Poetry is, I think, a more apt form than essays—at least the kind of essays that rely on strict rules of reasoning—for demonstrating what language can do.

We humans are these limited, embodied creatures that have developed different ways of making sense of the world: one way is reasoning, and another is through our bodies. Feelings link the physical body and the conscious mind in mysterious ways.

Poetry is tapped into the mystery. Like Ratatoskr the squirrel trotting up and down the world-tree, poetry flashes from body to mind, mind to body, bearing its messages.

Logical reasoning is important, of course. But I think we might put too much importance on the type of thinking that tells us the world is limited, dualistic, ordered, and so on. Perhaps we need practice developing and trusting—not *fearing*—other kinds of thinking. I feel, in my clearest moments, that the space around me is wilder than that. In fact, when I look inside myself, beyond my ego and masks, I see very little, or nothing: no name, or identity, or self. On a dusk walk, my hold over who I am is beautifully tenuous. Is this what Blake meant in *The Marriage of Heaven and Hell* when he asked, "How do you know but ev'ry Bird that cuts the airy way, / Is an immense world of delight, clos'd by your senses five?"

Lynch's *Mulholland Drive,* by ending in Club Silencio, points beyond language and away from the tidier connect-the-dots ending of *Oz.* Lynch leaves us in the potentially uncomfortable *inner room.* He doesn't place the reality of forms higher than freeplay.

Yet the ending of *Oz* is also satisfying perhaps because we've just experienced how much richer and more colorful the world of freeplay is.

The dream has brought color to "Kansas."

III.

Charles Simic sometimes begins his poems with a literal context (lost glove on a mailbox, doll's head on a beach, country fair) and then, winking at us time and again, he slowly reveals that it has all been surreal, freeplay. Such poems exists in a realm of imagination, dreams, interiority.

The title of Simic's long poem, "White," leads us to think that it will perhaps be about race, or snow, or even milk. Something white, surely. But he keeps shifting one white scene for another, baiting and switching. First, a shepherd in the Arctic Circle, then, "Someone like Bo-peep. / All her sheep are white." While the Arctic shepherd is possible (albeit unlikely), the nursery rhyme character disrupts the believability of the context. As a result, we cannot quite *see* the scene, or how it's white. That is, we can both see it and not see it. That frisson. Simic continually makes us think we see a literal image ("A white-out . . ."), then figuratively pulls it away ("In the raging, dream-like storm").

It's as if the speaker were trying to describe something specific, but it keeps coming out in a twist. So perhaps the poem is less concerned with white, as a color or concept or feeling, than how hard it is to talk about anything at all.

> As if I shut my eyes
> In order to peek
>
> At the world unobserved,
> And saw
>
> The nameless
> In its glory.
>
> And knew no way
> To speak of it,
>
> And did, nevertheless,
> And then said something else.

Just like Dante, who did "not dare / attempt" to describe the flaming brightness of the Virgin Mary, Simic admits that he is unable to speak about "The nameless / In its glory." Perhaps the color white, too, is Simic's approximation of a vision he had in his *inner room?*

> One has to make do.
> Make ends meet,
>
> Odds and ends.
> Make no bones about it.

Make a stab in the dark.
Make the hair curl.

Make a door-to-nowhere.
Make a megaphone with my hands,

And call and make do
With the silence answering.

He can't name what he's seen. Simic's original image (quintessence of white?), after being dragged from *inner room* across the *limen*, became too corrupted, altered, weird. The poem, in describing a thing-not-made-of-words (qualia, in philosophy: the internal and subjective part of sense perceptions), ends up enacting the writing process itself. The impossibility of it. The invention required. The white-out of silence. The white of the page.

By the end we feel that "White," in the Derridean sense, is just language. Unmoored, unleashed from reality. A space where, figuratively speaking, anything can happen.

When I begin to read a poem in my *room*—sitting in my chair, gulping coffee that makes my fingers and toes tingle—I don't immediately feel the *inner room*. I seek, through the poem, a *limen* that can lead me to the markers, the blazes, the thread. I long to go back in.

Simone Weil: "If only I could see a landscape as it is when I am not there. But when I am in any place I disturb the silence of heaven by the beating of my heart."

If Dōgen is right and No-Self is our essential nature, then there is no me. That is, at my base I am not substance, but silence. If the ecosystem of my *inner room* is silence, then moving from *room* to *inner room* is to go from body to no body, or from body to silence. It's the process of seeing a landscape without me in it.

Passing from *inner room* to *room,* my beating heart disturbs the serenity of No-Self. The body imposes itself on silence.

As Derrida perhaps helps us to see, we learn to threshold-cross through continual creative exploration. Over and over—separating seed from chaff, a process that reveals the inner core—we crack the pod and find the seed missing, which can be profoundly liberating. To discover that all the little petty parts of myself are illusory. My ego-inflated desire to be a "great poet," my jealousy of others' success, my desire for posterity, unreal!

I find myself asking, is *room* any more real than *inner room?* Surely not. Somehow, like nesting dolls, we've contained all the rooms the whole time.

You stand on a bridge in the mist. Stars above, black lagoon below.

Water splashes both shores. You breathe the mist.

One side: tall forests, snarling creatures. The other side: a city, burning.

You are in each world and neither. Feeling both on the skin.

Step forward (which way?) one of the ways.

To the burning city. Not burning, glimmering. In sunlight.

Philadelphia. Not glimmering. Crumbling, ash.

THE ELEPHANT OF SILENCE

Je suis maître du silence.
   —Rimbaud

I.

At fifty years old—summer 2020, Covid-mania white hot—I drove
my 1989 BMW motorcycle from Philadelphia to the Hambidge
Center in the mountains of northeast Georgia for a three-week
writing residency. They provided a cottage in the woods, with a wall
of windows and ample space for a "mad scientist" artist to spread
out their work.

My first feelings, after taking off my jacket and sitting down, were—
as Wendell Berry describes an arrival in a new forest—"along with
the feelings of curiosity and excitement, a little nagging of dread." It
was so damn quiet.

I've always felt a resistance to quiet. I was a hyper only child, never sitting still. The kid with firecrackers and toy soldiers. The teenager with the boom box. As an adult, I'm a talker and—I wince to admit it—a loud one. "Silence," as William S. Burroughs said, "is only frightening to people who are compulsively verbalizing."

In my humble opinion, I'm qualified to write an essay about silence precisely *because* I compulsively verbalize. I'm the least silent person in the room. I observe silence from the outside looking in. With the least "natural" perspective on the matter of anyone you know.

The Elephant of Silence built a house beside the sea. It contained all you'd need, including a bed and fine teacups. He liked to wash teacups and stare at the sea out the window. His radio cackled, *"The Last Forest contains 8,609 trees. A great number, albeit less than last year."* As he replaced the dishrag, he noticed an odd scene out the steamed window: a bride in white washed up on the surf.

There came a knock. He opened his door. A bride stood there, dripping wet, beside her pet pig. He invited them in. The bride burst inside and, with effort, lifted the Elephant of Silence off the ground, as if he were her groom. Her legs trembled. She groaned. Held there, his feet off the ground, the Elephant of Silence waited patiently.

The sun was setting. The pet pig stared at them with open admiration. Soon the bride was pancaked under the Elephant of Silence.

The pet pig butted him with his snout for pure joy. "Shall we go for a walk?" he asked. The Elephant of Silence packed them a picnic lunch. That night they slept in the Last Forest and their dreams were tinted spinach green. Next morning, they began climbing the mountain. It took them 2,000 years. Dynasties fell. The forest vanished behind them.

At the peak of that foggy mountain, the Elephant of Silence spoke, at last, with reverence: "I've never, in all my years, met another as silent as you."

The pet pig, weak as he was, performed one imperfect backflip.

They sat side by side, looking more or less like one another. They might have been the last two creatures in existence for all they cared.

I wrote that in 2012 after I started living with Tiina. The Elephant of Silence is Tiina, I think. In retrospect, it's unmistakable. She's from Finland, where folks value calmness and tranquility over storytelling and faking it till you make it. I've been to gatherings in Finland where a group of friends sit for extended periods in complete quiet. I've sat with men in saunas where none of us say anything; they just sip beer, happy as the day they were born.

When there's a gap in the discussion, I'm the one who panics and fills it with small talk. It's taken me years with Tiina to grasp the importance of leaving space during a conversation, for everyone to collect their thoughts.

It might go without saying that I'm the pet pig, following along beside her, learning from her.

By myself in the forest at Hambidge, I'm reminded of a retreat I went on thirty-one years ago, in 1989, at twenty. I had just decided that I was a writer, and figured I should have some alone time with my poems. On my father's 1975 Ducati motorcycle, I drove four hours from Halifax to our old camp in Bear River, where my parents and I had lived for a year when I was a kid. I intended to stay a week.

The camp, five miles from town and a quarter mile in the woods, was no longer the cozy candle-lit gingerbread house of my childhood. It had been adapted by neighbors into a hunting shack. The stove, which used to sit under the window, someone had shoved aside so they could lean a rifle on the sill. When a deer showed up, alert and curious, they'd shoot it. The gentle spirit of the house was gone.

Nevertheless, I arrived in Bear River full of gusto, with a sheaf of empty pages to fill with poems. I was set on finding inspiration deep in the forest. What I found, instead, was *silence.* And loneliness. I was alarmed. Feeling acute aversion, I wanted to escape.

Stubbornness kept me from returning home the same day I arrived. I had, after all, bragged to friends about the writing retreat I was going on. So—for one day—I sat in the armchair, read a long awful novel a girl had leant me (Sidney Sheldon, *If Tomorrow Comes*), wrote one poem, slept, and sped home.

Longest day of my life.

I always knew being quiet had value. But it's hard. I resisted.

Despite the noise I generated, I did grow up in a culture of silence, of a sort. My parents were hippies, meditators, readers. Our house contained walls of books on Eastern mysticism, Buddhism, Sufism. Novels, nonfiction, comics, math texts. There was space in the house for contemplation and wonder.

As an only child, I was often in my room playing chess by myself; reading comics; waging war with toy soldiers. Was I quiet at those times, or humming and singing to distract myself?

When I became a writer, I didn't think it would have anything to do with silence. But it does.

Over the days at Hambidge I settle into a routine, making peace with the quiet. Since it's my weakness, I sit with it, try to face it. I meditate.

Walk *slowly* in the forest, mindful not to obsess about ticks, bears, rattlesnakes. As the dread diminishes, I'm calmer. My focus deepens.

I love the feeling of quiet pooling, when I give it space. I get downright hungry for quiet.

After days of quiet, even the calm, socially distanced communal dinners—populated by seven congenial artists, the banjo player from Atlanta, the sculptor from Arkansas, the painter from Spain—seem jarringly noisy. Eager to return to my cottage, I walk briskly in the semidark, shut the door behind me, lie on my back, and stare into nothingness till I feel like myself again.

One morning, while I'm lying on the couch puzzling over a poem, there's a movement outside. A deer at the edge of the deck. Brown on green. Infinite gentleness.

I sit up straight. She sees me, goes still.

Ears high, aimed at me.

The cottage is never silent. The bones of the house creak, tic. Birds chirp outside. The fridge, now and then, hums. Cars on a near road make an oceanic whooshing. And there's my tinnitus: constant buzzing in my left ear from the rock concerts and discos I overindulged in, in my thirties.

Quieted, other quiet moments from the past drift by, on ice floes.

Waiting tables in a restaurant in Temple Bar, Dublin, August 1998, at noon the day after the Omagh bombing. To honor the dead, we were quiet for one minute. In that packed room, not a glass clinked.

Sitting by myself on desert sand outside Las Vegas, 1992.

Hanging upside down from a tree in Bear River, 1975.

Seated at dinner with my parents, thousands of times, holding hands before supper.

II.

Where does a poem come from? Silence, which includes quiet, contemplation, focus, oblivion.

Silence:

1. Absence of sound; *quiet*
2. Stillness; calmness; meditation; *contemplation;* imagination; dreams; the inner world
3. Fascination; sustained absorption; *focus*
4. *Oblivion*

These four aspects of silence are a vital part of the artmaking process. Like the underglimmer gates, we pass through these mind states in different orders, at different speeds, depending on who we are on a particular afternoon. Stillness might happen before quiet. Contemplation and focus might mean the same thing. Some dream, others "think."

SILENCE of QUIET

The word "quiet" means hushed, peaceful. When I say silence, I often mean quiet. Poems bubble up out of me when I'm hushed; when my mind is fertile, soft, malleable, open to the imagery around me. If I allow myself the luxurious time and space to slow down and focus—with that intention, listening actively—poems spring up out of the cobwebs.

First comes my intention to be quiet. I shut my eyes. I find a spot under a tree. I quit my job pouring drinks in a disco (Dublin, again). I buy earplugs.

Once we *want* quiet, it walks beside us. Nearer than we'd thought.

The Elephant of Silence is seated in the middle of the room, his great trunk wrapped around my chair. The Elephant of Silence *is* the room.

I did not say the poems spring up out of me, for I—my feeble psyche—am not the wellspring. Poems arrive like deer. If I'm quiet, they sometimes surprise me with a visit. If I leap up to grab them, they bound away.

SILENCE of CONTEMPLATION

Stillness trails quiet. Now you're sitting, facing the window, not tapping your foot, not fidgeting. Breathing slow, deep.

Contemplation is an impulse toward stillness, and vice versa.

You're no longer running through a crowded market *just to get through it,* but walking slow, breathing, pausing to look at the bearded human on a unicycle. You're riding a bicycle rather than driving. You're sitting by a lake rather than riding a bicycle.

You're the dreamer. One foot in the Lethe, the roaring death-stream of poems.

With contemplation, images percolate, formlessly. The inner cities flash with lightning.

Some religions, like Hinduism and Buddhism, suggest we use a mantra—a sacred utterance (like *Om,* or ॐ), considered to possess mystical qualities, repeated with eyes closed—to calm down. To some extent, I think, the good relaxing feeling derived from mantras, or from making art, comes from minimizing internal thoughts and external stimulus, and from maximizing focus.

Focus brings discipline to stillness. Focus brings form.

I'm sitting by the lake, a cloud catches my eye. Rather than just look at the next cloud (or my phone), I center on that cloud, let it pool, see where it leads. Does it look like a fractured boat sinking into the blue? Is it Coleridge's "painted ship"? Or Franklin's ship, trapped in the blue ice of the Northwest Passage?

One can contemplate on a noisy street, with focus. Silence is possible within noise.

John Cage's composition *4'33"* (1952) is about silence but not the lack of sound. His score instructs performers to take their places and not to play their instruments for four minutes, thirty-three seconds. The piece consists of the sounds listeners hear while the performance lasts.

Fostering contemplation and focus, we find form. Every artwork—no matter how *vers libre* it seems—has form. In Cage's piece, the form is the length of time, the performance space, the musicians, the audience, the time of day, the light.

SILENCE of OBLIVION

Oblivion is the limbo-feeling I sometimes get if I stare too long into the night sky. It says that I am an insignificant speck on the face of the earth, that my life and my poems are meaningless.

It's the feeling, I presume, that scared me at twenty in the forest of Bear River. A feeling of lonesomeness bordering on worthlessness.

But if we hold the feeling of oblivion, and don't resist it, its wisdom emerges. For, truly, aren't we insignificant specks on the face of the earth?

In the seventeenth century, John Donne liked to imagine himself "*coffind*," as he called it. He slept in a coffin, and even posed for an artist to engrave his funeral monument. Such a reminder of oblivion, putting our brief lives into perspective, is surely restorative.

But we should not sleep in a coffin for too long! Oblivion can become quicksand that sucks us down and leaves only a husk.

THE GREAT SILENCE

The 1968 Spaghetti Western *The Great Silence* (*Il grande silenzio*), directed by Sergio Corbucci, animates the notion of oblivion.

It's a sublime revenge narrative. The hero, Silencio, is the fastest draw in the West. When Silencio was a child, bandits cut his throat—leaving him mute—and killed his parents. In the film, he hunts them down.

The Great Silence takes place in winter: vast white vistas swallow up the tiny towns. People freeze in snow, drown in frozen lakes. Everyone shivers. Death is close.

Corbucci leads us to think that the great silence is God, in the form of Silencio the savior. But at the end, the gang of bad guys (led by Klaus Kinski, with nasty charisma) murder the good guys, including Silencio.

How refreshing! And uncomfortably realistic. The great silence, it turns out, is death, coming up the driveway for the good folks and the bad.

Although the mute gunslinger in *Il grande silenzio* (1968) is called Silencio, the silence of the title refers to death.

III.

Allowing our wounds to surface (contemplation), and sitting with those wounds long enough to write them down (focus), requires stillness and quiet and patience.

If we impatiently (viz. *noisily*) tell the poem what to say, then the good parts (the cloud "magically" turning into Franklin's ship) might not have a chance to emerge.

We artists love the recognition, what little comes to us. But, from my experience, the true reward of making art occurs in hushed moments when a tricky poem I've been working on suddenly slips into place. Such a moment always feels like a gift. It can occur while alone or with others, with or without noise. Just slip your head, turtle-like, back into your shell and there is the concentration, the silence, the offering.

Such silence is the source of the work, its theater, and its portal of transmission to the reader.

David Lynch describes, in his nonfiction book *Catching the Big Fish,* how meditation has been a tool for him to become the person and artist he is. The big fish, he says, is the great idea, the line, the vision, the film. We bring ourselves to the water and wait for the big fish to break the surface.

We cannot force the big fish to come. We can only live a life that allows for the best possibility of glimpsing it.

A simple, ancient notion. When we're peaceful and calm, the work appears. Or, as Rumi puts it: "Out beyond ideas of wrongdoing and rightdoing / there is a field. I'll meet you there. // When the soul lies down in that grass / the world is too full to talk about."

The deer visits me again. I'm reading, facing the big window.

I watch, not moving. I don't lower the book.

We're both completely still.

PARADISE LUDIC

Mir ward Alles Spiel.
  —Nietzsche

I.

The kid tosses the ball into the air and—

When I was sixteen my new girlfriend, Linda, told me, "John, you're a funny guy!" Emerging from years of acne and self-doubt, I took this as a tremendous compliment. The jokester role suited me. I realized that, without being aware of it, I'd developed a sense of humor, as a way perhaps to avoid a certain kind of tension with my parents.

At university I embraced this jokester identity: a disguise to help me mingle with the intimidating professors and sharp-tongued students. As we read "serious" work like *The Waste Land,* I thought, this is great but isn't it missing something? I'd grown up reading *Archie* comics and loving inane movies (*1941, Stripes*) and sitcoms (*Happy Days, Three's Company*). I wanted art to accommodate the "lowbrow" wit I was familiar with: goofy pratfalls, savage satire, irony. I loved the Porter in *Macbeth,* pretending drunkenly that he's arrived at the gates of hell: "Here's a knocking indeed! If a man were porter of hell-gate, he should have old turning the key." How great, making jokes that undercut every authority, in the shadow of the dead king!

I loved tragedy, but not when the tone was unironically solemn and heavy. I couldn't stand the dreary Victorians (Arnold, Tennyson, Carlyle), particularly when a metronomic meter was used to cheer the high ideals of British colonialism (Kipling). But the wacky absurdist playwrights—especially Ionesco, Beckett, Pinter, Genet—I could really get behind.

In Ionesco's *Rhinoceros,* everyone in a French village—except the main character, Bérenger—slowly turns into a rhinoceros. The play seems to lampoon French citizens that capitulated under the German occupation of WWII. But, more importantly to me, *Rhinoceros* is fun. Everyone but Bérenger talks in clichés, so the context seems to disintegrate before our eyes. Ionesco wrote with such high energy and silliness, I laughed out loud as I read it! He wasn't borrowing authority from form or tradition. There was underlying meaning and substance, but it didn't make a big deal out of itself. It seemed to be appealing to me directly.

Soon after, I found Joyce's *Ulysses,* Stein's *Tender Buttons,* and Ted Hughes' *Crow.* I had a new criterion: my literary heroes should be able to make me laugh.

Johan Huizinga, in *Homo Ludens,* suggests that play is a vital part of society: even within its serious institutions, like religion, judicial proceedings, war, and philosophy. Huizinga argues that the ludic (Latin: *ludus: game,* or *play*) exists at all levels in all cultures and is primordial. Since animals played before humans, it precedes culture.

According to Huizinga, play must have five characteristics:

1. Play is free, is in fact freedom.
2. Play is not "ordinary" or "real" life.
3. Play is distinct from "ordinary" life both as to locality and duration.
4. Play creates order, is order. Play demands order absolute and supreme.
5. Play is connected with no material interest, and no profit can be gained from it.

At the center of Huizinga's definition of the ludic is *fun*. Fun happens in a field or game arena: a closed microcosm in which "performance is its own end," and only the game makes sense. Games and play overlap, becoming a single voluntary, non-utilitarian, fun concept, conducive to physical creation, emotional creation, and re-creation: "play is a voluntary activity or occupation executed within certain fixed limits of time and place, according to rules freely accepted but absolutely binding, having its aim in itself and accompanied by a feeling of tension, joy and the consciousness that it is 'different' from 'ordinary life.'"

Play is ubiquitous, mystical, indescribable. Since all culture has a play element (within it, and also distinct from it), the boundaries between playful and serious are often blurred and become quickly irrelevant.

Even "the structure of the creative imagination itself" is, according to Huizinga, evidence of play. Poetry, he says, shows how forms can be playfully manipulated: "In the turning of a poetic phrase, the development of a motif, the expression of a mood, there is always a play-element at work." Poetry and play are, to Huizinga, almost identical twins: "Play, we found, was so innate in poetry, and every form of poetic utterance so intimately bound up with the structure of play that the bond between them was seen to be indissoluble."

A traditional, academic essay is no place to express the ludic. It's perhaps the least playful mode of communication in existence. The least fun. The ludic is irrational, mercurial. Verb, not noun. Metaphor, not verb. A five-paragraph essay cannot hold the ludic any more than New Orleans can hold a storm; the ludic swirls across the essay, leveling paragraphs in its wake. Nor can a mind hold it. The ludic pushes against the confines of what we know, metastasizing, bursting into new shapes. To capture even a small part of it, we've got to let go of the forms we usually rely on to communicate.

Many essays these days are breaking the mold. New breeds of do-or-die nonfiction. Bizarre, vernacular, poetic nonfiction—such as Bernard Suits' *The Grasshopper* (1978), Mary Ruefle's *Madness, Rack, and Honey* (2012), Brian Blanchfield's *Proxies* (2016), Zach Savich's *Diving Makes the Water Deep* (2016)—clearly demonstrating that the form is thriving.

Huizinga was a scholar interested in showing, rigorously and systematically, how the ludic is built into the patterns of human behavior. I am a poet, an artist, fascinated by how the ludic moves in the artwork I love, and by how it might inspire our creations.

For Huizinga, the child best encapsulates the ludic. "To understand poetry," he says, "we must be capable of donning the child's soul like a magic cloak and of forsaking man's wisdom for the child's." He meant, I think, children's innate sense of fun, of rejecting authority, of inventing games. Kids are natural iconoclasts. But an iconoclast—"One who assails or attacks cherished beliefs or venerated institutions on the ground that they are erroneous or pernicious"—seems to know *why* they are rejecting authority, while the child is interested in fun at all costs, irrationally, impossibly. The child has an intuitive sense of disrupting serious human activities. "Without play," says Peter Brooks in *Seduced by Story,* "we risk being overwhelmed by an inhuman world." Such rejuvenating play, Brooks points out, can be seen in children's games:

> Watching children do 'let's pretend' games, filling imaginary teacups and driving imaginary cars, often with very few props, it is clear that while completely absorbed in making things up they are also aware that it's all make-believe. They can step out of the make-believe in order to add new props or new situations to their play; a new playmate arrives: 'he can be the father'; some new object comes to hand: 'let's pretend this is the engine for the train.'

In mythology, tricksters—boundary-crossers who defy conventional behavior—encapsulate the child's inborn sense of the ludic. Nanabozho, in many First Nations stories (particularly Ojibwe), takes the shape of ravens, coyotes, hares, making mischief and breaking rules. As the Joker tells Harvey Dent in *The Dark Knight* (2008): "I'm like a dog chasing cars. I wouldn't know what to do if I caught one. You know, I just do ... things."

The ludic destroys and creates, creates and destroys, over and over. A game "destroys" the space it's in by introducing a new order, new rules. It annihilates structures and generates new ones. The outcome is uncertain, messy.

Imagine if, during an NBA basketball game—a "serious" sport with eight-figure player salaries, executives, managers, coaches, agents, advertising—a man peeled off his clothes and streaked across the court. The streaker destroys (briefly) the NBA game, imposing another idea (perhaps climate change) and another order (the game of "Streak"!). Certainly, to me, the streaker represents a deeper form of play than the scheduled-years-in-advance billion-dollar basketball game. More spontaneous, funner, wilder. But who am I to privilege one game over another?

Another example: a young protester duck-walks past a row of police officers, thus "destroying" the authority of the police: imposing another idea, another order, onto the scene. The duck-walk ends quickly and will not be further articulated. But—if only for a millisecond—the duck-walk *is* a new ludic order, moving toward its own rules, its own system: separate from ordinary life, profitless, *free.* As Huizinga says, play wants rules, wants order. But it will not always achieve or fully articulate that order.

When I make a poem, it destroys the silence around it. It interrupts the white page and also the ethos of my apartment in West Philadelphia, by creating its own sounds, its own ink, its own ontology. "*Poiesis,* in fact, is a play-function," Huizinga says. "It proceeds within the play-ground of the mind, in a world of its own which the mind creates for it. There things have a different physiognomy from the one they wear in 'ordinary life,' and are bound by ties other than those of logic and causality."

William Blake is well known for the unrestrained mythic worlds of his poems. In *Songs of Innocence and of Experience* (1789), Blake contrasts the state of protected innocence (e.g., "Infant Joy") with the "fallen" world and its institutions (e.g., "Infant Sorrow"). His *Songs of Innocence* addresses the inherent spirituality of the child, while *Songs of Experience* depicts the fractured psyche of the adult.

Some of the children in Blake's illustrations for *Songs of Innocence*— as in "The Echoing Green"—play on the vines and trees at the edges of the frame: an act of literal frame-breaking. Implying, I think, that children have the ability to transcend the corporeal world and ascend to the level of divinity. Reaching out of our world and into the next.

II.

Directed by Luis Buñuel, *Simon of the Desert* (*Simón del desierto,* 1965) is a short (forty-five minutes) surrealist allegory, full of ludic silliness and rich satire, about a fifth-century Syrian Catholic saint, Simeon Stylites, who lived on top of a column for thirty-seven years.

The ascetic, up on his column, seeks to prove his devotion to God in the face of temptation by the devil. Mexican actor Claudio Brook, as Simón, is hilariously zealous and befuddled, never quite cracking a smile.

Acolytes come from miles around to visit Simón. All seem to depart unsatisfied. A poor man who's had his hands chopped off asks for new hands, so Simón mumbles a few words and the man's hands magically appear. The man, ungrateful, wanders away without a word of thanks. Two onlookers dismiss the "miracle" ("See that?"

The setting for 90 percent of *Simon of the Desert* (1965): Simón high on his pedestal, under a big empty sky.

"What?" "That thing with the hands." "Oh, that.") So Buñuel under-cuts, with child-like glee, the church's notion of hagiographic marvels.

The Mexican desert, for Buñuel, is a kind of existential backdrop, like a painting by Dalí (they were frequent collaborators, most famously on the 1929 film *Un chien andalou*). Using close-ups and wide crane shots, Buñuel creates a huge and symbolic scope for his allegory. The camera is usually far below Simón, on the ground, to evoke a sense of reverence. Simón, arms constantly outstretched to the skies, seems both mocking and transcendent.

Buñuel, rather than keeping his central character mysteriously dis-tant (*à la* Gatsby in *The Great Gatsby* or Kurtz in *Heart of Darkness*), keeps shifting to Simón's perspective, to his doubts and silly ponder-ings, as well as his constant parroting of holy verses. Simón comes off as absurd, stilted, unholy.

The large crowds below Simón evoke in us, first, a sense of faith and devotion, until Simón forgets his prayers and talks nonsense to them. When Matias, a fresh-faced priest, offers Simón food, the ascetic says he has enough food "with the lettuce God gives me." He chastises Matias for having clothes that are *too* clean, which is a sin. When Matias walks away with a smile, Simón calls him an idiot. Later Simón criticizes him for not having a beard, resulting in Matias being ejected from his monastery.

Out of nowhere Simón calls out to the sky, "Until thou callest me to thy side, I'll use one leg only to support my body." So he stands on one leg like a flamingo for the remainder of the film.

A dwarf goatherd, after chatting with Simón, tells his goat, "I've got a feeling he's not quite right in the head."

"Eternity," Heraclitus wrote, "is a child playing, playing checkers; the kingdom belongs to a child."

Nietzsche responded (two and a half millennia later), "And as the child and the artist play, so too plays the ever living fire, it builds up and tears down, in innocence—such is the game eternity plays with itself."

In *Thus Spoke Zarathustra,* Nietzsche outlined three progressive stages of human development: the camel, the lion, and the playing child. The camel carries a burden, the lion howls in wrath. The playing child, for Nietzsche, is the culmination of the human spirit. Once the playing-child stage is achieved by an individual, the disruptive, illogical, natural, innocent force of play can be used as a powerful instrument to disrupt traditional values and modes of operation within culture.

As adults we have to be mature, to stand in lines, to be patient with other citizens. But being an adult can be corrosive if we never have a break, if we take it too seriously. The seriousness of being an adult needs balance, levity, reprieve. *Fun.* Peter Brooks points to Schiller's notion that "Play . . . allows humans to fulfill their nature: 'man only plays when he is in the fullest sense of the word a human being, and *he is only fully a human being when he plays.'*"

Through "the ever living fire" of the child's game, we can burn off— even momentarily—the nonsense of adulthood and return to a more authentic self. Making art is one way for us, as adults, to uncover and retain our artist-child side. Brooks: "[Children] are, as Paul Harris puts it in *The Work of the Imagination,* in a world of 'half-belief,' and I think that state of mind and emotion carries over into adult enjoyment (and writing) of fictions."

"Man," Heraclitus says, "is most nearly himself when he achieves the seriousness of a child at play."

Nietzsche's playing child contains two important characteristics: first, he builds and destroys; second, he's free of moral ends. The game has its own morality, separate from the outside world. The "innocent" child is immersed in the playing of the game—just "chasing cars," as the Joker says—without concern for repercussions.

When Alfred Jarry's frenzied play *Ubu Roi,* a parody of *Macbeth,* was performed at the Nouveau-Théâtre in Paris in 1896, people rioted in the streets. The first word—*"Merdre!"* ("shit" in French, with an extra *r*), spoken by Firmin Gémier as Père Ubu—was followed by fifteen minutes of booing and jeering. For these traditionalists, the unruly, obscene, bizarre vision was too much. So Jarry—building up and tearing down, the serious child at play—poked his unruly finger at the "adult" theatergoers of *Fin de siècle* Paris.

It would be hard to call Buñuel's film amoral. We sense the Nietzschean playing child in action, but there's also a moral end, for sure. The moral is both mysterious and distinct. Buñuel is taunting the deadly serious Catholic Church: their saints, history, institutions.

What if—Buñuel asks, tongue firmly in cheek—Simón isn't so smart, or his dreams involve lust, or he isn't sure what the hell he's doing? Is he still saintly? And if not, what does that say about the church, about faith itself? Buñuel, with childish fun, destroys church customs over and over, reframing them in front of our eyes into another order: *the film.*

The central tension of Buñuel's film, from which the surrealism arises, comes from Simón's four encounters with the Devil, played with ferocious glee by Silvia Pinal (who also, four years earlier, played the unironically devout nun in Buñuel's *Viridiana*), looking very anachronistically mid-1960s and blonde. The Devil's modus operandi: attempt to lure Simón off his pedestal through increasingly disturbing disguises.

Simón and the Devil Meeting #1

The Devil, grinning slyly, walks past Simón's plinth in silence carrying a jug on her shoulder. She has weird hairy hands, long horny nails. Simón doesn't notice.

Simón and the Devil Meeting #2

Out of nowhere the Devil appears in a Bo Peep outfit, pushing a hoop with a stick, scream-singing: "Thou, son of rabbit-ridden Syria! You good man, Simón! With the lovely thick beard! And teeth brushed clean WITH SYRIA'S URINE!" She skips aggressively, flirting and taunting at the bottom of the plinth. "What," Simón asks, "are you doing here?" She answers, coyly, "Playing."

Ferocious Silvia Pinal as the Devil: telling Simón what a lovely beard he has, licking it, and then sticking him with a hatpin.

When she shows Simón her long legs, complete with stockings and garter belt, and bares her breasts, he finally understands that she's the Devil, and piously raises his hands back up to the sky. She pops up beside him, licks his moustache, sticks him with some kind of hatpin, and turns into a naked old woman running away on the sand yelling, "I'll be back, shaggy locks!"

III.

In the twentieth century, a host of ludic writers exploded in the wake of Joyce. But great literature has a long history with the ludic: Aristophanes, Rabelais, Gogol, Lewis Carroll, and countless others.

Blake is a prime example of a playful poet who is often thought of as "serious." Just look at the sketch he made to accompany his well-known poem "The Tyger":

Songs of Experience: The Tyger. William Blake, 1794. Relief etching printed in orange-brown ink and hand-colored with watercolor and shell gold. Perhaps Blake—creating this image five years after the poem was first published—added the goofy expression to cast doubt on his unironic poem?

The poem is about the destructive power of God, asking who but God could create a beast as ferocious as the tiger. But the tiger in Blake's illustration, far from terrifying, resembles a stuffed animal. The illustration is unsatisfying if we approach the incantatory poem with "adult" seriousness, but it's delightful on a ludic level! It also play-fully undermines the implicit threat of the poem's final statement—"Tyger Tyger burning bright, / In the forests of the night: / What immortal hand or eye, / Dare frame thy fearful symmetry?"—by daring to "frame" the tiger.

Blake's longer works, like *Jerusalem* and *Milton,* while being daunt-ingly difficult to enter, are also quite ludic. Blake, like Buñuel, seemed to want to destroy certain traditional values to discover what was hidden underneath. After working hard to understand Blake's basic narrative and sense, readers unexpectedly find themselves initiated into the vast universe of his imagination: a riotous, illogical, mythic space ruled by the playing child.

Simón and the Devil Meeting #3

Christ—who is obviously Pinal the Devil wearing a curly wig and fake beard and clasping a real-life lamb—appears. She tells Simón, "Come down off that column, taste earthly pleasures till you've had your fill. Till the very word pleasure fills you with nausea!" She gets so keyed up that she dropkicks the lamb.

When Simón finally recognizes that it's the Devil, she hits him with a rock, yells "I'll be back shaggy locks!" and explodes into dust.

John Milton—a political dissenter who attempted in *Paradise Lost* (1667) to redefine political, religious, and personal freedom on an epic scale—was Blake's hero, but that did not keep him safe from Blake's satire.

In his visionary epic poem *Milton* (1810), Blake drags Milton back to life to make him pay for two "mistakes" he'd made. Milton was, Blake thought, 1. a misogynist who depreciated women, particularly his wife and daughters; and 2. flawed by his heavy reliance on what Blake called a Urizenic (Blakean pun: *"your reason,"* that is, authoritarian) God. Milton's overreliance on reason made *Paradise Lost,* in Blake's estimation, into a simple reconstruction of the old oppressive system of the Bible, rather than the revolutionary poem it should have been.

In *Milton,* Milton is called back down to earth from Beulah: a sleepy, sexual place where people rest if they are not ready for the pure creativity of spiritual Eden. On earth, Milton must learn the nature of his errors and discard them. He finds himself in a deadly struggle with Urizen:

> Urizen emerged from his Rocky Form & from his Snows,
> And he also darkend his brows: freezing dark rocks between
> The footsteps. and infixing deep the feet in marble beds:
> That Milton labourd with his journey, & his feet bled sore
> Upon the clay now chang'd to marble; also Urizen rose,
> And met him on the shores of Arnon . . .

Arnon—a river in the mountains of Gilead, referred to in the Bible—means "rushing torrent." "The shores of Arnon," according to Blake scholar S. Foster Damon, symbolize the female genital tract. If we accept this interpretation, the wrestling match between Urizen and Milton could be Blake's way of pushing Milton's face, figuratively speaking, into the error of his ways. According to Blake, Milton showed respect for love, but erroneously considered love inferior to reason.

Blake's carnivalesque imagery makes people who think they are superior to women, but who are then squeamish when it comes to sexuality, seem laughable. A child's prank! Such imagery, in the world of "high" literature, is refreshingly lowbrow.

It's worth noting that Blake, in his way, also depreciated women. His wife Catherine lived in his shadow for almost fifty years, modeling and printing for him, and existing in his poems spectrally as Enitharmon, wife of the "eternal prophet" Los, and as the poet's "shadow of delight" in the second part of *Milton*. One can only imagine what it must have been like for Catherine, putting up with the wild demands of a possibly psychotic poet for decades.

So Blake rewrites *Paradise Lost* the way he thought it should have been written in the first place: forcing Milton to learn a lesson, and releasing Milton from his self-imposed religious constraints.

There is, I would argue, also a deeper sense of the ludic in Blake's work. Blake, in the Nietzschean sense, attempted to burn through the corrupt systems he saw around him, and replace them with "eternal" systems. Reprogramming his reader, he hoped, from a flawed way of thinking to a visionary one.

Blake ends *Milton* with a kind of apocalypse which he calls The Great Harvest. This is not the final apocalypse of Christ's second coming, but a purging of surface forms, unveiling the spiritual life beneath. The Harvest is made possible when people acquire spiritual vision, as Milton does. When an individual transcends the narrow parameters of human perception, they, like Blake's eternals, open their eyes to the endless play of spiritual possibilities.

> loud groans Thames beneath the iron Forge
> Of Rintrah & Palamabron, of Theotormon & Bromion, to forge the
>   instruments
> Of Harvest: the Plow & Harrow to pass over the nations.

At the Harvest, all people, "the Oppressor and the Oppressed," will sit down, drink together, and experience "the sports of love, & . . . the sweet delights of amorous play." Nietzsche might have thought of it as casting off the camel and the lion.

Blake, it's worth noting, assigns limits to play. For him, vision is an eternal truth that supersedes the ludic. In "A Vision of the Last Judgment" he says, "Vision or Imagination is a Representation of what Eternally Exists, Really & Unchangeably." Thus, the function of the visionary imagination is—like the children climbing out of the frame in "The Echoing Green"—to get *beyond* the images of the ordinary world to the eternal forms they represent.

"Striving with Systems," as Blake's alter ego Los does in *Jerusalem,* "to deliver Individuals from those Systems."

The game arena, Huizinga tells us, is a sacred place. An opportunity for spiritual re-creation. In *Simon of the Desert,* Buñuel's most blasphemous moments contain something close to what I would call mysticism. Simón, up on one leg on his plinth, puzzling over the shrieking Devil below him, is both ridiculous and sublime.

Clearly, then, the ludic is also, in some sense, "serious." But why can't play be serious and also not serious? Each example of art that I love—by Buñuel, Blake, Vigo, Marker, etc.—have moral undertones. None of my examples—aside from the Joker, who might truly be nihilistic—entirely fits Nietzsche's criteria of being free of moral ends.

Buñuel playfully mocks Simón's asceticism, as Blake mocks Milton's. But Buñuel is also *not* playing. Throughout his career, Buñuel, a Marxist, mercilessly ridiculed the institutions that supported bourgeois morality. He was critical of Franco's dictatorship in Spain and lived much of his life in exile from his native Spain as a result.

Huizinga tells us, unsatisfyingly, that the ludic exists "beyond seriousness": "If a serious statement is defined as one that may be made in terms of waking life, poetry will never rise to the level of seriousness. It lies beyond seriousness, on that more primitive and original level where the child, the animal, the savage, and the seer belong, in the region of dream, enchantment, ecstasy, laughter."

I'm not sure the matter needs to be so cut and dry. Why can't the ludic be both sober *and* plastered?

The Italian filmmaker and poet Pier Paolo Pasolini is a good example of an artist who succeeded in pushing the extremes of play and also moralism. Pasolini's film *Salò, or the 120 Days of Sodom* (1975) is savagely ludic in its attack on fascist values. This "satire" includes extreme violence, sadism, and torture.

Yet even Pasolini's notion of the ludic had limits. Describing himself as "an unbeliever who has a nostalgia for a belief," Pasolini also directed (and wrote the screenplay for) *The Gospel According to St. Matthew* (1964). This film—in contrast to Buñuel's, which doesn't allow its holy ascetic Simón much dignity—is a respectful depiction of Christ in which he heals the blind, raises the dead, and exorcises demons. Pasolini, in creating such an unironic portrait, seems to have thought Christ beyond the limits of the ludic.

That restless "play-sphere"—the freeplay space that poets access, in which the playing child destroys and reconstructs—is not just fun but also critical and crucial. This was, I think, Williams' point when he said, "It is difficult / to get the news from poems / yet men die miserably every day / for lack / of what is found there."

Simón and the Devil Meeting #4

A coffin slides impossibly through the desert, halting at the foot of Simón's column. The top pops off and the Devil is inside, wrapped in a blanket, one breast uncovered. She materializes next to Simón on his plinth.

"Get ready to leave, Simón," she rasps. "I'm taking you to the sabbath. There you'll see tongues of flame and the gaping red wounds of the flesh. Enough! Let's go. They're coming for us."

A modern passenger airplane, high above, flies toward them in that fifth-century sky.

The scene shifts: a modern city, disorienting skyscrapers, a bridge, an urban street. A nightclub, rock band on stage, electric guitars, teenagers dancing, shimmying, gyrating, arms flailing. It's the 1960s! The Devil and Simón are beatnik hippies watching the kids dance. Simón, sporting a little Leonard Nimoy beard and useful cardigan, puffs a pipe.

The Devil gloats, triumphant. The dance floor "sabbath" is *her* scene.

Simón accepts this vision of hell, wearily.

—another kid runs out of nowhere, grabs the ball, and it starts

EPILOGUE

Tarkovsky's *Stalker* haunts me. In the visionary Zone, Stalker lies be-side a river; the shot pans slowly, meticulously, over the water. In the shallows we see a syringe in a metal box: objects we recognize from earlier, on the nightstand in Stalker's room. So Tarkovsky blurs the line between inner and outer. By the river, are we in Stalker's inner psychic space? Or is his presence perhaps affecting the outer makeup of the Zone itself? As with Glück's talking flowers, Lynch's dreamers, and Buñuel's saints, the threshold between interior and exterior is constantly traversed.

Cocteau asked us to imagine what the cinema of poets could be. I haven't mentioned "Ode to a Nightingale," but while writing this book I kept thinking of the little indie documentary about John Keats that was filmed in the fall of 1819. INSERT SHOT: close-up on Keats—at twenty-three, fine brown hair, hazel eyes—standing very still at the edge of the forest, utterly absorbed. "Darkling," he purrs, gazing just above the camera, "I listen; and, for many a time / I have been half in love with easeful Death . . . " The film could have featured, if Keats had been unavailable, Anne Carson, Amiri Baraka, Lorca, or maybe Bashō!

Silence is hard to talk about. Confronted by that sense—while, some-times, looking at a sunset, or a Rothko painting—of existing within some greater infrastructure, I was surprised to find myself leaning, over and over, on Buddhism, particularly Tibetan and Japanese traditions. I'm a novice Buddhist, at best. But Buddhist language is useful to help grab hold of ephemeral ideas. What is the way to write a poem? In a koan, a monk asks Master Haryo, "What is the way?" Haryo replies, "An open-eyed man falling into the well."

Of course, the ephemerality of certain concepts, like the underglim-mer, is what led me to puzzle through them in the first place. After all, scratching the surface of any art form—passing through form and content to what's beneath—leads to surprising depths.

I've tried, in every case, not to disturb the depths and silence with noisy explication. If Goya was right that "fantasy abandoned by rea-son produces impossible monsters," then we curious bystanders best keep a respectful distance. Goya continued: "United with her [i.e., reason], she [i.e., fantasy] is the mother of the arts and the origin of their marvels." A delicate ecosystem holds reason and fantasy in bal-ance. The last thing the monsters need are tour guides in their lairs and mazes. I've tried, as Fellini does at the end of *La dolce vita,* to leave each *mostro* in peace, without poking it with my critical stick.

I'm hoping, most of all, that folks who find themselves wandering into these essays with me contribute to the conversations around them through their own creative acts. Follow the blazes, as Jack Gil-bert calls them, into their own psyches. Perhaps they'll find, down there in the semidark, a blue-haired lady in a box seat whispering, *"Silencio."*

Selected Bibliography & Filmography

The ideas in this book started out as marginalia—musings, doodles, poems, lists—that I wrote in pencil in the books I loved. Writing an essay, I become a marginalia hunter. Retracing my steps toward a half-remembered passage, I usually find, amid my jumble of dog-eared books and scattered notes, something more inspiring along the way. This bibliography is my best attempt at compiling the books and films that inspired me while writing these essays.

SELECTED BIBLIOGRAPHY

Adorno, Theodor W. *The Culture Industry: Selected Essays on Mass Culture.* Ed. J. M. Bernstein. Routledge, 2001.

Aristotle. *Aristotle: The Poetics.* Harvard University Press, 1960.

Artaud, Antonin. *The Theater and Its Double.* Translated by Mary Caroline Richards. Grove Press, 1958.

Ashbery, John. *Houseboat Days.* Viking Press, 1977.

Bachelard, Gaston. *The Poetics of Space.* Translated by Maria Jolas. Beacon Press, 1994.

Bakhtin, M. *Rabelais and His World*. Translated by Iswolsky Hélène. Indiana University Press, 1984.

Baraka, Amiri. *SOS: Poems 1961–2013*. Grove Press, 2015.

Barthes, Roland. *Camera Lucida: Reflections on Photography*. Translated by Richard Howard. Hill & Wang, 1981.

Bashō, Matsuo. *The Narrow Road to the Deep North*. Penguin Books, 1966.

Beckett, Samuel. *Endgame and Act without Words*. Grove Press, 2009.

Berger, John. *Ways of Seeing*. BBC, 1972.

Blake, William. *The Complete Poetry and Prose of William Blake*. Anchor Books, 1997.

Blanchfield, Brian. *Proxies*. Nightboat Books, 2016.

Bolster, Stephanie. *Long Exposure*. Palimpsest Press, 2024.

Brooks, Peter. *Seduced by Story*. New York Review Books, 2022.

Bunting, Basil. *Briggflatts*. Bloodaxe Books, 2009.

Carson, Anne. *Short Talks*. Brick Books, 1992.

Cocteau, Jean. *The Difficulty of Being*. Translated by Elizabeth Sprigge. Da Capo Press, 1995.

Coetzee, J. M. *Life & Times of Michael K*. Penguin Books, 1985.

Corral, Eduardo C. *Guillotine*. Graywolf Press, 2020.

Dahl, Roald. *The Wonderful Story of Henry Sugar and Six More*. Jonathan Cape, 1977.

Deleuze, Gilles. *Francis Bacon: The Logic of Sensation*. Translated by Daniel W. Smith. Bloomsbury Academic, 2017.

Derrida, Jacques. *Writing and Difference*. Translated by Alan Bass. University of Chicago Press, 1978.

Diaz, Natalie. *Postcolonial Love Poem*. Graywolf Press, 2020.

Dickinson, Emily. *The Poems of Emily Dickinson*. Ed. Thomas H. Johnson. Belknap Press of Harvard University Press, 1955.

Dillard, Annie. *The Writing Life*. Harper & Row, 1989.

Dostoyevsky, Fyodor. *Crime and Punishment*. Translated by Michael R Katz. W. W. Norton & Company, 2020.

Eliot, T. S. *Selected Essays: 1917–1932*. Harcourt, 1950.

García Lorca, Federico. *Poet in New York*. Translated by Ben Belitt. Grove Press, 1955.

———. *The Selected Poems of Federico García Lorca*. A New Directions Paperbook, 1955.

Gilbert, Jack. *Refusing Heaven: Poems*. Alfred A. Knopf, 2005.

Glück, Louise. *Proofs and Theories: Essays on Poetry*. Ecco, 1994.

——. *Louise Glück: Poems 1962–2012*. Farrar, Straus & Giroux, 2013.

Gogol, Nikolai. *Dead Souls*. Translated by Richard Pevear and Larissa Volokhonsky. Vintage, 1997.

Hafiz. *Hafiz of Shiraz: Thirty Poems: An Introduction to the Sufi Master*. Handsel Books, 2003.

Haines, John Meade. *Winter News: Poems*. Wesleyan University Press, 1966.

Hayes, Terrance. *American Sonnets for My Past and Future Assassin*. Penguin Books, 2018.

Heaney, Seamus (translator). *Beowulf: A New Verse Translation*. Farrar, Straus & Giroux, 2000.

——. *Finders Keepers: Selected Prose 1971–2001*. Farrar, Straus & Giroux, 2003.

Heraclitus. *Fragments: The Collected Wisdom of Heraclitus*. Penguin Books, 2003.

Hirshfield, Jane. *Nine Gates: Entering the Mind of Poetry*. Harper Perennial, 1998.

Hughes, Ted. *Crow: From the Life and Songs of the Crow*. Harper & Row, 1971.

Huizinga, Johan. *Homo Ludens: A Study of the Play-Element in Culture*. Beacon Press, 1980.

Ionesco, Eugène. *Rhinoceros, and Other Plays*. Grove Press, 1960.

James, William. *The Varieties of Religious Experience: A Study in Human Nature*. Modern Library, 1936.

Jarry, Alfred. *Ubu Roi: Drama in 5 Acts*. New Directions Books, 1961.

Joyce, James. *A Portrait of the Artist as a Young Man*. Ed. Seamus Deane, Centennial edition, Deluxe edition. Penguin Books, 2016.

Jung, C. G. *Synchronicity: An Acausal Connecting Principle*. Princeton University Press, 1973.

Kafka, Franz. *The Trial*. Penguin Classic, 2000.

Keats, John. *Selected Poems and Letters*. Ed. Douglas Bush. Houghton Mifflin, 1959.

Kelly, Donika. *The Renunciations*. Graywolf Press, 2021.

Ladislav Fuks, *The Cremator*. Translated by Eva M. Kandler. Karolinum Press, Charles University, 2017.

Larkin, Philip. *Selected Poems of Philip Larkin*. Faber, 2011.

Larrington, Carolyne (translator). *The Poetic Edda*. Oxford University Press, 2014.

Longinus. *On the Sublime*. Forgotten Books, 2018.

Longmire, Warren C. *Open Source*. Radiator Press, 2021.

Lynch, David. *Catching the Big Fish: Meditation, Consciousness, and Creativity*. Tenth anniversary ed. Penguin Books, 2016.

McCarthy, Cormac. *Blood Meridian*. Picador, 1985.

Nabokov, Vladimir Vladimirovich. *Nikolai Gogol*. New Directions Books, 1944.

Neruda, Pablo. *The Poetry of Pablo Neruda*. Farrar, Straus & Giroux, 2005.

Nietzsche, Friedrich Wilhelm. *Thus Spoke Zarathustra*. Cambridge University Press, 2006.

O'Hara, Frank. *The Collected Poems of Frank O'Hara*. University of California Press, 1995.

Olds, Sharon. *Strike Sparks: Selected Poems, 1980–2002*. Alfred A. Knopf, 2004.

Oliver, Mary. *Devotions: The Selected Poems of Mary Oliver*. Penguin Books, 2020.

Olson, Charles. *Selected Writings of Charles Olson*. Ed. Robert Creeley. New Directions Books, 1966.

Oswald, Alice. *Falling Awake*. W.W. Norton & Company, 2018.

Pasolini, Pier Paolo. *The Selected Poetry of Pier Paolo Pasolini*. Translated by Stephen Sartarelli. University of Chicago Press, 2015.

Passarello, Elena. *Animals Strike Curious Poses*. Sarabande Books, 2017.

Plath, Sylvia. *The Colossus and Other Poems*. Knopf, 1976.

Pound, Ezra. *The Cantos of Ezra Pound*. New Directions Publication Corporation, 1970.

Rilke, Rainer Maria. *Letters to a Young Poet*. W.W. Norton & Company, 1993.

———. *The Selected Poetry of Rainer Maria Rilke*. Vintage, 1989.

Rimbaud, Arthur. *Arthur Rimbaud: Complete Works*. Harper Perennial Modern Classics, 2008.

Ruefle, Mary. *Madness, Rack, and Honey*. Wave Books, 2012.

———. *Selected Poems*. Wave Books, 2010.

Rūmī, Jalāl al-Dīn. *The Essential Rumi*. Harper, 1996.

Savich, Zach. *Diving Makes the Water Deep*. Rescue Press, 2016.

Simic, Charles. *The World Doesn't End*. Harcourt Brace & Company, 1989.

———. *The Monster Loves His Labyrinth: Notebooks*. Ausable Press, 2008.

Smith, Tracy K. *Duende*. Graywolf Press, 2007.

Shapero, Natalie. *Hard Child*. Copper Canyon Press, 2017.

Stein, Gertrude. *Tender Buttons*. Penguin Classics, 2018.

Stevens, Wallace. *The Collected Poems of Wallace Stevens*. Alfred A. Knopf, 1954.

Strugatsky, Arkady, and Boris Strugatsky. *Roadside Picnic.* Gollancz, 2000.

Su, Adrienne. *Middle Kingdom.* Alice James Books, 1997.

Suits, Bernard. *The Grasshopper.* University of Toronto Press, 1978.

Suzuki, Shunryu. *Zen Mind, Beginner's Mind.* Weatherhill, 1970.

Tanahashi, Kazuaki, ed. *Enlightenment Unfolds: The Essential Teachings of Zen Master Dōgen.* Shambhala Publishing, 2000.

Tarkovsky, Arseny. *I Burned at the Feast: Selected Poems of Arseny Tarkovsky.* Translated by Philip Metres and Dimitri Psurtsev. Cleveland State University Poetry Center, 2015.

Tate, James. *Return to the City of White Donkeys.* Ecco, 2004.

———. *The Route as Briefed.* University of Michigan Press, 1999.

Tranströmer, Tomas. *New Collected Poems.* Translated by Robin Fulton. Bloodaxe Books, 1992.

van der Kolk, Bessel A. *The Body Keeps the Score: Brain Mind and Body in the Healing of Trauma.* Penguin Books, 2015.

Weil, Simone. *Simone Weil: An Anthology.* Grove Press, 2000.

Whitman, Walt. *Leaves of Grass.* Ed. Jerome Loving. Oxford University Press, 1990.

Williams, William Carlos. *Selected Poems.* New Directions, 1985.

Winters, Yvor. *Yvor Winters: Selected Poems.* Library of America, 2003.

Wordsworth, William. *The Major Works.* Ed. Stephen Gill. Oxford University Press, 2008.

Wright, Franz. *Walking to Martha's Vineyard.* Knopf, 2005.

Yamada, Koun. *The Gateless Gate.* Wisdom Publications, 2004.

Zapruder, Matthew. *Why Poetry.* Ecco, 2017.

SELECTED FILMOGRAPHY

Antonioni, Michelangelo. *L'avventura.* Cino Del Duca, 1960.

Buñuel, Luis. *Simón del desierto.* Sindicato de Trabajadores de la Producción Cinematográfica, 1965.

———. *Viridiana.* Unión Industrial Cinematográfica (UNINCI), 1962.

Clarke, Shirley. *Portrait of Jason.* Film-Makers' Distribution Center, 1967.

Corbucci, Sergio. *Il grande silencio.* Adelphia Compagnia Cinematografica, 1968.

Denis, Claire. *Beau Travail.* La Sept-Arte, Tanais, SM Films, 1999.

Eisenstein, Sergei. *Battleship Potemkin.* Goskino, 1925.

Fellini, Federico. *La dolce vita*. Astor Pictures Corporation, 1960.

Fleming, Victor. *The Wizard of Oz*. Metro-Goldwyn-Mayer (MGM), 1939.

Haneke, Michael. *Funny Games*. Concorde-Castle Rock/Turner, 1997.

Herz, Juraj. *The Cremator*. Barrandov Studios, 1969.

Hitchcock, Alfred. *Vertigo*. Paramount Pictures, 1958.

Hooper, Tobe. *The Texas Chain Saw Massacre*. Bryanston Distributing Company, 1974.

Hopper, Dennis. *Easy Rider*. Columbia Pictures, 1969.

Kubrick, Stanley. *A Clockwork Orange*. Warner Bros., 1971.

———. *The Shining*. Warner Bros., 1980.

Lynch, David. *The Elephant Man*. Paramount Pictures, 1980.

———. *Eraserhead*. American Film Institute, 1977.

———. *Mulholland Drive*. Universal Focus, 2001.

Marker, Chris. *Letter from Siberia*. Argos Films-Procinex, 1957.

———. *Sans Soleil*. Argos Films, 1983.

Martel, Lucrecia. *The Headless Woman*. Strand Releasing, 2008.

Nakata, Hideo. *Ringu*. Toho, 1998.

Nemes, László. *Son of Saul*. Hungarian National Film Fund, 2015.

Nolan, Christopher. *Memento*. Newmarket Film Group, 2000.

Norbu, Khyentse. *The Cup*. Palm Pictures, 1999.

Pasolini, Pier Paolo. *The Gospel According to St. Matthew*. Titanus Distribuzione, 1964.

———. *Salò, or the 120 Days of Sodom*. Produzioni Europee Associati, 1975.

Renoir, Jean. *Rules of the Game*. Gaumont Film Company, 1939.

Saura, Carlos. *Carmen*. Orion Pictures, 1983.

Schepisi, Fred. *The Chant of Jimmie Blacksmith*. Hoyts Theatres, 1978.

Tarkovsky, Andrei. *Mirror*. Mosfilm, 1975.

———. *Stalker*. Goskino, 1979.

Vigo, Jean. *À propos de Nice*. Macmillan, 1930.

Wachowski, Lana, and Lilly Wachowski. *The Matrix*. Warner Bros., 1999.

Weir, Peter. *The Last Wave*. United Artists, 1977.